The LIZARD LORDS

The LIZARD LORDS

Stanton A. Coblentz

AVALON BOOKS

THOMAS BOUREGY AND COMPANY, INC.

22 EAST 60TH STREET · NEW YORK 10022

PUBLISHED SIMULTANEOUSLY IN THE DOMINION OF CANADA
BY THE RYERSON PRESS, TORONTO

PRINTED IN THE UNITED STATES OF AMERICA
BY THE COLONIAL PRESS INC., CLINTON, MASSACHUSETTS

The LIZARD LORDS

CHAPTER I

No one was ever able to explain the three flashes of light that startled the small California town of Plummetsville on an otherwise peaceful June evening. They were of an uncanny purple flourescence and scarlet-tinged at the edges, and they followed each other a few seconds apart, wavered high in the western sky, then faded out as if at the turning of a switch. Observers declared that they bore little resemblance to meteors. Officials strenuously denied that any military aircraft were in the vicinity. And military men laughed to scorn the idea of the possible involvement of planes or spaceships from Russia or any other country.

The people of Plummetsville were still trying to account for the strange lights when, three days later, they were stunned by another mystery. Popular young Ted Hilary, son of the town's leading banker, Judson J. Hilary, and a student in chemistry at Cranshaw University, had suddenly disappeared. And with him a young woman had vanished: twenty-year-old Eileen Vernon, who had come to town only last fall to teach in Cartwright Union Junior High. The two had last been seen at about four on the afternoon of June 18, as they wound side by side up a footpath through the tall hills just to the west of town. Often before, Ted and Eileen had been observed arm in arm; and it was whispered that their engagement would soon be announced. Hence no one was surprised to see them go rambling off together. But their acquaintances were alarmed when they did not return that afternoon or night, nor the next day, nor the day after, and when searching parties scoured the hills without reporting any trace of the missing pair.

"Sure looks to me like foul play, boys," Police Chief Michael Y. Callahan confided to members of his staff. "I'm going to lead the hunt myself. We'll comb every root and stone of them there hills!"

Two days later, no evidence had yet been found. And then, on June 21, Plummetsville was awed by a third mystery. The Police Chief too had disappeared!

There was no coherent account of how it had happened. Lieutenant Jim McGrogan, who had been accompanying the Chief, reported that he and Callahan had been tracing some suspicious footprints in wild Manzanita Canyon, about five miles from town. Suddenly something—McGrogan could not say what—drew the Chief behind a clump of bay trees, whose dark-green foliage screened him from sight. McGrogan thought he heard a grunt or a gasp, which he attributed to some passing animal. But after several minutes, when the Chief had still not returned, the lieutenant grew impatient. He called out, but received no answer; then peered behind the bay trees. There, on the twig-strewn ground, McGrogan saw what he thought to be the signs of a scuffle, though later observers could detect no such evidence. The one fact agreed upon by all was that Callahan had disappeared.

It was at this point that Judson J. Hilary, incensed at "the brainless idiocy of the cops," moved into the case on his own behalf. By means of a long-distance call, he engaged the services of George Orson Harwood, the nation's best-known private detective, whose ingenuity had solved several celebrated cases, including the Gruggiano murder and the Wellington jewel robbery. It was now foreseen that, within a few days, the mystery of the three disappearances would be solved. Harwood, taking command, was said to be pursuing an entirely new line of inquiry, which was taking him deeper than the police had hitherto probed into the wilderness west of town.

It was while plumbing this wilderness that he himself became involved in the most stunning mystery of all. Plummetsville and the entire country gaped in amazement when on June 26 the news came to them of a fourth disappearance.

"We don't know how or when it happened," Deputy Sheriff Hal Trevor reported. "We'd seen him only a little bit before, but when we looked again, we couldn't find no more trace than if he'd jumped right off the Earth."

Trevor was referring to the famous detective, George Orson Harwood.

As Ted and Eileen set out together, the day was warm and scented. But as they wound through the eucalyptus grove and out across a brown field of wild oats, the long curling fog-streamers began to blow in across the redwood-covered hills to the west. This was by no means unusual at this season, for the ocean was but two miles away; and the mist did not dampen the spirits of the young pair, who laughed and chatted until they had reached their favorite nook, a wide leaf-strewn open circle, beyond which the tall redwood spires arose above dark-leafed bay trees and rosy-barked madronas.

"You know, sweetest," said the girl as she threw herself down beside the trickle of clear water known as Fern Creek, "I feel almost that forces from some other world are right at our elbows!" She was a slim, sprightly redhead, with intense deep-blue eyes that sparkled vivaciously; and the quick, vehement gestures of her long, thin form showed the vividness of the life within her.

The man's black eyes, as he stood staring down at her out of tortoise-shell glasses, flashed sudden fire. He was tall and black-haired, with a long, keen mobile face, and his movements, like hers, were lithe and rapid. "Forces from some other world?" he answered. "So long as you're here, dearest, forces from this world are quite enough for me!"

He let himself down on the soft earth beside her; his arms reached out. The fog that had made a gray ceiling above them, draping out the treetops, seemed a gentle protective covering. But as his arms went about her waist, the girl threw him off, and leapt up.

"What's that?"

"What's what?"

He, too, was on his feet, scanning the dim edges of the forest for the chance hiker who might have been spying upon them.

For a few seconds, neither spoke.

"I—I—I don't know what it was," she gasped, giving her shoulder-long red hair an excited toss. "I—I—you'll think I'm crazy when I say—well, when I say it was just like something out of a storybook. Like a big lizard, with a long tail, but very pale, almost a shadow. It was taller—well, taller than I am, and it faded out like a light you've turned off. I—I'm afraid, Ted!"

She clung to him, and his arms enclosed her. But the immense fog-capped trees, the wide, open hollow and the peaceful little stream seemed to give no reason for alarm.

"Nonsense, Eileen!"

Hardly were these words out of his lips when the fury struck. Neither of them could ever say quite what had hit them. It was as if they had been swept up in a whirlwind, flung about, blown away, hurled through space in a nightmare. He attempted to call her name, but the words seemed caught in his throat. He had lost track of her, and she of him in that gray whirling blankness, which seemed to last a long time.

Then they heard clattering sounds, followed by a swishing and threshing. And suddenly, as if blinders had been pulled off their eyes, they could see.

"God have mercy!" cried Ted, dragging one hand in amazement across his forehead.

A moan just to his left drew his attention to a wide-eyed, white-faced girl.

"Are you—are you all right?" he gasped.

"Are you?" she groaned back.

But neither answered. Neither ever had words to describe what they now saw and felt.

"Dearest," he said, "we've been kidnapped."

"By whom? Where are we, Ted? *What* has happened?"

The man's answer was a long, staring silence. *Where,* indeed, were they? *What* had happened? Were they only dreaming?

They stood in an odd closed compartment, on a floor that swayed gently, like the deck of an anchored ship. The place was pervaded with a faint mist, and with a peculiar pungent odor that brought reminders of oil of cloves. The curving walls, not more than about seven feet high, were clothed in a woolly, glowing purplish substance, which also coated the floor and the inverted U of the ceiling. There were no windows, no furniture, and no source of light except the purplish glow. The compartment was long, perhaps seventy or seventy-five feet, but when Ted started forward in a dazed way to explore it, some uncanny force stopped him after about a dozen feet.

Strangely, it was not like a physical force. It was like an order that thundered in his mind, "Go back! Go back! Go back!" Still more strangely, he could not disobey—he had no wish to disobey.

"Hope you're not seeing things too, Eileen?" the man questioned, his big dark eyes wide with concern.

She looked up at him confidently out of her strained lovely face. Impulsively she pressed close to him. Her whole form trembled.

Then, acting on their common thought, he began looking about him for ways of escape in the apparently unbroken walls. Into his alert mind a suspicion had come—one too fantastic to be confided even to her.

Even as he wrestled with his fears, a peculiar snapping sound issued from the wall to his rear, and he swung about with a start just in time to see a sort of dark metal shelf shot out by a mechanical arm.

"My God!"

The shelf contained two long, flask-shaped, coppery vessels filled with a clear liquid, side by side with several brown loaf-shaped objects, each one longer than his hand.

"Where—where'd it come from?" the girl burst out, in a shaky voice. "What, in the name of—"

She was cut short by slow, sonorous tones, spoken in a peculiar low-pitched foreign accent, and proceeding as if from the empty space just before them.

"Eat and drink! You will need food and drink for the long voyaging ahead."

"Who—who the devil—" Ted cried, knowing that his reeling, unsteady sensations were not due entirely to the rhythmic rocking and swaying in the walls about him.

He was never to finish his sentence.

For the fraction of a second, Eileen's shriek diverted his attention. Then he saw what she was pointing at—something so strange, so grotesque that he backed away instinctively.

Facing him at no more than about three yards, there was a nightmare creature. Well over five feet tall and all covered with shimmering silvery scales, it was lizard-shaped, with long arms each tipped with seven-clawed hands, and a thick body which, standing almost upright on its two seven-clawed legs, ended in a long flat tail. Its wedge-shaped head glittered with four variously colored eyes, one pair placed far forward, and one behind; a fifth eye blinked weirdly near the tip of its tail. Half a dozen waving octopus-like tentacles, six to eighteen inches long, twisted and waved between the narrow orifices of the ears and nose, which lay level with the face. The mouth was wide and toothless, the heavy lips of a bluish tint.

As the prisoners, clutching one another in their fright, stood staring at this apparition, a startling transformation came over the creature. It grew paler, its silvery hue gave way to a pearly glow, then to lemon yellow, and then to almost every other color from bright orange to palest lavender, and from jade-green to glimmering pink, while firefly flashes appeared and faded in its tail-eye. Then suddenly it vanished.

"Be not surprised, Earthlings," they heard the slow, sonorous tones droning, with a sepulchral quality. "I am still here. We Drumgradians would rather be heard than seen."

"Drum what?"

The girl had pressed back against the wall, where she clung to her companion frenziedly.

"Drumgradians. People of Drumgrade, who is a nearby world, locationed not even a thousand light-years away in the system of the sun Prokepsis, in what you Earthlings know as the constellation of Hercules."

Both hearers, listening to the careful yet faulty English, were dumbfounded.

"It may give you much surprise to hear your own language spoke by a man from another world," the voice went on, mispronouncing some of the words. "We Drumgradians, being able to make ourselves unvisible, have long time been moving among your people, studying your ways, listening to your speech, learning it, and practicing it by ourselves. That is our way whenever we come to a new planet for specimens."

"Specimens?" Ted shouted. "You call us specimens?"

He had started forward as if to throw himself upon the Drumgradian. But how fight an antagonist whom you cannot see?

A grating, rhythmical noise, which sounded suspiciously like laughter, came from a few feet away, accompanied by a clattering as the monster moved about.

"You—you vile—you beastly—" Ted broke out.

"Call me Orneppu," the creature interrupted, still with that grating, which resembled laughter. "My name, she is Orneppu. You will need to tell me from my companions."

"Oh, God!" cried Eileen. "So you're not the only one?"

"There are only two others. You will meet my brothers—when they wish it."

In a near-swoon, Eileen had slumped down to the purple-covered floor. And while Ted bent anxiously over her, the unseen droned on:

"You wonder how we Drumgradians have unvisibleness. That is simple. The chemistry of our bodies, she differs from yours. She is not based on carbon but on silicon. Therefore her main substance has resemblings to glass or plastics that let the light through them. Also, we make unvisibleness by organs which use the light as we see fit, taking from it any rays including ultra-violet and infra-red, so as to give us the color we please, or else hide us from view."

Eileen and Ted were hardly listening. While the girl recovered from her faint and staggered back to her feet, the man started forward once more, fist swinging.

"Tell me," he demanded, "where are we? Why are we here? What do you intend doing with us?"

Again that rhythmical grating, resembling laughter.

"You will know everything—in time," stated Orneppu. "You are in the spaceship whose name I may translation as *Great Galaxy*. It is anchored safe under the sea, so that your people will not discover it, for it cannot be made unvisible."

"Anchored under the sea? *Under the sea?*" Now Ted understood that swaying and rocking which had been puzzling him. At the same time, he realized the impossibility of escape.

"Yes, we are safe under the sea!" echoed Orneppu's deep, solemn tones. Briefly he revealed himself in a coppery glow, while his long flat tail threshed slowly about on the floor and his vehemently waving tentacles gave off sparks.

"Eat and drink, my friends," he invited, pointing with one sharp-clawed hand to the dark metal shelf, with its food and drink. "You have a long, long voyaging ahead!"

CHAPTER II

"What on Earth do you think, dearest, they mean to do with us? When—oh, when can we get out of this?"

For a moment Ted was silent, having no answer to the girl's impetuous question. Already, according to his wristwatch, more than twenty-four hours had passed since their capture, and they were no nearer than ever to solving the mystery—and no nearer to escape.

"Well, this at least is clear," he analyzed slowly. "If that devil Orneppo or Orneppu and his pals meant us any harm, they wouldn't go out of their way to care for us." After all, he reminded the girl, they had each been given a little sleeping cubicle, where, amid folds of the woolly purplish substance, they might be fairly comfortable. And they had been provided with bathing and sanitary facilities of a sort, along with food that seemed nutritious enough.

"That clear liquor in the flask-shaped vessels," he pointed out, "well, it tastes about like shadow soup, but there's something concentrated about it—a very little seems to satisfy my hunger and thirst."

"Yes, and that bread," she added, with a grimace toward the brown loaf-shaped objects on the metal shelf, "I suppose it's edible, though its flavor reminds me of baked clay."

"Guess we'll have to get used to it," Ted muttered. "What irks me is to be locked up like a convict." For the fiftieth time, he started forward experimentally. And for the fiftieth time, he was halted by an invisible barricade.

"Oh, dearest, what will our friends be saying?" wailed the girl. "They'll be looking for us everywhere — Heavens, what's that?"

They were both startled by a strange lurching and shuddering. After a minute or two, while they had the impression of being jerked upward, they heard a jarring from above, as of a door being forced open. At the same time, a breath of fresh air burst upon their nostrils. To their ears there came a splashing sound. Their eyes caught a glimpse of the stars.

But between them and the stars, so filmy that the constellations shone through it, they made out a darting lizard shape, which vanished in an instant, while the splashing seemed to increase. Then they heard a banging as of a lid being slammed down, the stars disappeared, the splashing ceased, and they felt themselves sinking back to their former position.

"What—what do you make of it, dearest?" asked Eileen, her big deep-blue eyes wide with horror.

"Make of it? Clearly one of those demons—or maybe more than one—has been taking a little jaunt outside."

"But wouldn't he be drowned?"

"No such hope, I'm afraid. Most likely his body is

lighter, more buoyant than ours, and it wouldn't be much trouble for him to swim ashore. Of course, he chose the nighttime so that this confounded vessel wouldn't be seen. But what the devil is he up to?"

"Nothing good, you can be sure," sighed the girl.

Less than twenty-four hours later, her pessimism was confirmed. Again there came a lurching and shuddering, and they had the impression of being jerked upward. Again they caught a breath of fresh air as a partition in the roof was opened, while a lizard shape was vaguely outlined against the stars. But beside this shape—or, rather, clutched in its arms—they saw something bulkier and darker, which dropped to the floor of the ship like a sack of rocks.

"Look, Ted! Look! A man!" cried Eileen, as the bulky object thumped to rest on the floor beside them.

It was, in fact, a very large man, and he wore a blue-black uniform, and lay immobile as a corpse. As they bent over him, Ted and Eileen gasped in recognition.

"Well, I'll be damned!" Ted muttered, observing the round red face with the pug nose, wide lips, and prominent chin.

Eileen had gone white. "Is he—is he dead?" she gasped.

"No, I don't think so." Tentatively Ted felt the unconscious man's forehead, which he found to be warm. He was reaching for the left wrist when once more they heard that deep, sonorous voice which they had grown to expect and detest.

"Have no fear, Earthlings. We have sent him to sleep. We have done this with the gas we call Clerovox. One whiff—she is sufficient. She kills most sensationings, so that the Earthling makes no foolish resisting. You both had Clerovox before we brought you to our ship."

The man and girl, bending over their fellow victim, hardly heard these words. Callahan, they saw, was twitching slightly. He groaned, muttered a curse, brushed one hand in a bewildered way across his face, which seemed ruddier than ever before; then opened his small, brown-flecked gray eyes.

"Holy Mother! Where am I?"

His startled look, as his gaze met Ted's and Eileen's and then traveled about the glowing purple walls, was that of a man still in a dream. Automatically his right hand reached toward his pistol-belt. But the holster was empty.

"Come, take it easy, man," counseled Ted, noticing the confusion on the Chief's grizzled face. "You're going to be all right."

"Where—where in hell do *you* come from?" Callahan threw out in a husky voice.

He raised himself to a sitting posture, stared at the pair like a man out of his wits, groaned again, and sank back.

"By gum," they thought they heard him mutter, "I've sure gone nuts!"

But after a moment, he sat up again, and looked about him, still in bewilderment.

"Them thugs must have jumped me from behind," he managed to explain. "I was in the woods, following the trail of you folks, hunting for clues, when all at once everything turned black." He growled to himself, and staggered to his feet. "Lord's sake! What a hangout for them gangsters!"

After stumbling forward a few feet, he stopped short, the astonishment on his big round face deepening. He too had been halted by the mysterious unseen.

"Stay where you are, Earthling!" ordered a squeaky voice out of the invisible, which, the prisoners would learn, belonged to a companion of Orneppu named Mervex. "The rat in a cage, she cannot escape!"

Callahan reached again for his revolver, having seemingly forgotten that it was gone.

"We took that criminal weaponing from you," rumbled Orneppu, "so that you could not hurt yourself. When our specimens reach Drumgrade, they must be strong and whole."

"Drumgrade? Drumgrade?" shrilled Eileen. "What under heaven do you mean?"

There was no reply except that grating sound like derisive laughter.

Nor were they to have any answer for several days. The coming of the naturally cheerful Callahan did much meanwhile to relieve the monotony. "Don't you folks worry," he would say, his red face widening in a genial grin, while he would unbare his right arm and flex and unflex its powerful muscles. "Look, folks! It's just like iron! Thirty-five years I've been on the force—thirty-five years, folks, last March—and never the man I've seen what could get the best of me. We'll find a way to beat this bunch of hoodlums, believe me! Unless I miss my guess a thousand miles, Jim McGrogan and the boys are hot on their trail right now!"

Three days more, according to Ted's wristwatch, crawled by without event, while he spent hours in ranging back and forth on an eight-foot space of the swaying floor. Then at last they heard a sound like a door rattling open above, caught a whiff of fresh air, and briefly saw the stars. "Looks like they're out after more big game!" Ted decided grimly.

Surely enough, within another twenty-four hours, the door in the roof opened once more, and an unconscious figure dropped to the floor.

The newcomer, who groaned and slowly revived, was a man of about forty, with a tall, slim form, a greyhound face beneath the trim, well-combed, dark-brown hair, a cinnamon-colored tweed suit immaculately pressed, and deep-set, screwed-up eyes that, from beneath their bushy brows, surveyed the surroundings with a puzzled and suspicious air. Over his left shoulder a little black case, hardly larger than a fair-sized book, was slung on a strap.

"Where in perdition am I?" he gasped, glaring at Callahan with accusation in his glance. "What's happened? What is the meaning of this?"

Then, as the mists cleared from his mind, his gaze took in Ted and Eileen, who were bending over him anxiously.

"Name of the devil! I—I—" he burst out, forcing himself half erect; and seemed unable to finish the sentence. "You two—you two—unless I've gone dafter than a loon—you're the missing pair!"

Ted and Eileen, feeling that the man's intense greenish eyes were looking right through them, introduced themselves.

"How'd you know we're the missing pair?" Ted asked.

"How'd I know? Isn't it my business to know? Haven't I examined every photograph of you till I was blue in the face? You don't know me, of course, but

Mr. Hilary engaged me to conduct the investigation. My name's Harwood."

"Harwood? Not George Orson Harwood?" chorused the three hearers. For, of course, everybody had heard of the celebrated detective.

"This plot has wide ramifications—much more so than I'd suspected," Harwood decided, rising and stretching his long arms until he could touch the glowing purple ceiling. "Evidently there's a whole gang. Still, I've never seen any gang headquarters like these. There must be big money—"

The detective broke off, started back as if ready to collapse. He thought he had seen an immense lizard that darted against the farther wall like a shadow and vanished.

"There is *not* big money!" denied Mervex, who had evidently been eavesdropping. "My brothers and I—we are not like the crime-doers of your planet. We have a higher purpose when we collector our specimens."

Again that word "specimens," which always sent a chill down the hearers' spines.

"Truly, a higher purpose," affirmed Orneppu's rumbling tones. "You should be flattered, you four, to be the chosed ones."

"But what are we chosen for?" Ted almost shouted.

"That I must not say—not just yet," slowly answered the unseen. "But some things I can explain, so as to readify you for what lies ahead. Sit down on the floor, all of you!"

A strange-looking company the captives made, Ted seated next to the girl, one arm protectively around her shoulders, while the huge, uniformed, crimson-faced shape of Chief Callahan flanked them just to the right, and George Orson Harwood sat a little apart to the left, his darting eyes ranging the compartment as if to ferret out every detail, his lean, well-manicured fingers opening and closing nervously.

Even as he spoke, Orneppu had made himself visible again, in the very act of peering into the black case slung over Harwood's shoulder, from which he turned with a puzzled glance as containing nothing to interest him. Now all listened intently as, in the deepest tones yet, he broke into speech.

Fascinated, the prisoners stared at the big lizard form nearly upright on the two great legs, the waving tentacles, the seven-clawed hands, the five eyes, the wedge-shaped head, the long flattened tail, and the body that changed color with bewildering rapidity amid firefly sparks from the tail-eye.

"Earthlings," Orneppu's slow, resonant voice droned forth, "did you see the three bright—what do you call them?—purple flarings when we came to your planet?"

Somehow his gaze was fastened upon Chief Callahan. And Callahan almost automatically replied.

"Sure we saw three bright purple flares. But how in blazes could we know you'd come to our planet?"

With a swift gliding movement, Orneppu stalked before the watching company. His tail gave an emphatic smack against the floor. Beside him the smaller, slimmer, orange-spotted form of Mervex was momentarily visible.

"Purple," Orneppu went on, "she is the color of Drumgrade, which we use in all ceremonialings. Your friends will see three more flarings tomorrow when we leave."

"Tomorrow? When we leave?" Ted gasped. "You don't —you can't mean to say—"

Orneppu shone in a greenish light, faded out, and reappeared in a red glow.

"I would not say it if I did not mean to say it!" he snorted. "That is why, Earthlings, I want to readify you."

An awed silence followed. Eileen stared at Ted apprehensively, while he reassuringly pressed her arm.

"Tomorrow we leave for Drumgrade," the speaker rumbled on, with a gesture of one seven-clawed hand toward Harwood. "Now we have all the specimens we can carry back safely."

Ted had staggered to his feet, his black eyes blazing. His tall form lunged forward threateningly. "This—this—" he stormed. "You can't do this!"

"We *can!*" Orneppu asserted, with rasping laughter, while his opponent was stopped short as by an invisible wall.

"Now, Earthlings, listen!" he went on. "You will like Drumgrade. It is—what is your word for it?—almost your sister world, with a plentiness of sunlight, water, and oxygen. You will feel at home."

"What do you intend doing with us?" demanded Ted. "How can you get us to your world? Didn't you say it was a thousand light-years away?"

Strange glitters came into Orneppu's front eyes, and his tail-eye flashed queerly.

"Well, not quite. By your Earthling count, only about nine hundred and—"

Ted groaned. "Even traveling at the speed of light, we'll be dead long before we get to your planet. Even our great-great-grandchildren's great-grandchildren—"

A purplish glare in the Drumgradian's front eyes brought Ted to a halt.

"You talk like a child!" Orneppu grumbled. "What do you Earthlings know of anti-time and anti-space?"

"Anti-time? Anti-space?"

"That is the best way I can speak it in your language. The old space-travelings, of course, are much too slow even for Drumgradians, though our lives are ten times more long than yours. We still use primitive ways, which you call atomic energizing, to begin and end a voyaging, and to light and heat us. But most of a voyaging is made like the winking of an eye in anti-time and anti-space."

Ted had sunk back on to the floor beside Eileen. All stared in a questioning silence at Orneppu, whose color had changed to a flickering blue, through which the glowing purple walls were visible.

"It is hard to make the explaining," Orneppu went on, struggling more than ever before to express himself. "Your language, she has not the words. Well, let me ask—have you heard of anti-gravity and anti-matter?"

For the first time, Harwood spoke up. "As theories only!"

"With us, we call them facts. Think of this. Everything in the world has two sides. There is day and night, heat and cold, sleep and waking, the neutron and the proton, life and death. In the same way, time and space have two sides. When you have a dreamless sleeping, you are in anti-time. When your thoughts fly thousands of miles, you are in anti-space. This, of course, is only in a crude way."

"Is it—well, like being on another dimension?" questioned Ted.

Orneppu's front eyes flashed a bright yellow.

"Not at all! It is like being on no dimension—or on an anti-dimension. All direction and all extension disappear. You can go anywhere in time or space. You must, however, regulation your voyaging so you can leave anti-time and anti-space at the right point. But this we can do by a machine, which I may call the Anti-Spacifier. Tomorrow, my friends, you will see more about all this."

As if realizing for the first time the dread threat hovering over them, the four prisoners were suddenly on their feet. Eileen, trying hard to stifle a wail of protest, bent her head and began weeping silently. Callahan let out a roar and turned redder than ever, while his huge fist beat the air. Harwood, more restrained, coughed slightly from a cold he had just contracted, and muttered curses beneath his breath. Meanwhile Ted, with a baffled expression, merely stared at their oppressor's lizard form, which suddenly faded out.

As Orneppu vanished, Harwood began pacing the narrow confines of their gently swaying prison, though he too was barred as by an invisible wall from moving forward more than a few steps.

"It's some sort of electronic gimmick—clever, I'll say!" he reasoned. "There's still a lot of things I haven't figured out. How, for example, did those conspirators get us all here underseas, yet not one of us got wet?"

"I put that question to Orneppu," stated Ted. "His answer, as far as I could make it out, was that we were carried from shore in some sort of a self-propelled collapsible small boat—a submersible, apparently."

"Never heard of such a boat!" grunted Harwood. And then, halting in his slow pacing of the floor, "Why can't we get hold of one of those boats ourselves, and escape in it?"

"Swell idea!" joined in Callahan. "Trouble is, we don't know where them gangsters keep them, and wouldn't know how to use one of the darned things if we did find it. Besides, that big five-eyed lizard—I ain't what you'd call superstitious, but if he ain't the devil himself—"

"Devil—like my old grandmother!" snorted the detective, scornfully. "Oh, I don't deny, Callahan, there's scientific wizardry in it, all right, but it's plain as daylight it's nothing but some complicated sort of stage contraption, most likely with the help of TV—"

He was interrupted by the sudden reappearance of Orneppu, who waved his tail with its blinking eye as if in mockery, then flitted out of view.

"So you don't believe," asked Ted, "that Orneppu and his gang actually intend taking us to another planet?"

"Do *you* believe it?" growled Harwood. "Of all the nonsense—and I've heard a lot of it in my time, believe me—this anti-time and anti-space take first prize. Can't you see it's just a bunch of hokum meant to scare us?"

"Then why—why are they holding us here?" plaintively asked Eileen, giving her thick mat of red hair an anxious toss.

The detective's sharp greenish eyes surveyed her with a sort of amused contempt. He coughed before replying, as to a child who persists in ridiculous questions, "My dear young lady, maybe you've forgotten that the father of your betrothed, Judson J. Hilary, is reputed to be a very wealthy man. Maybe you've never heard of such things as kidnappings for ransom. I'll admit that this gang is the keenest and boldest I've ever run across. That's a darned original idea, locking their prisoners under the ocean in a submarine—and with all this stage scenery, too! But as soon as old Hilary comes to terms with them—and if I'm any judge of men, he'll go to any limit to save his son—they'll let us all out unharmed!"

"Oh, I hope so! I do hope so!" fervently answered Eileen.

Ted and Callahan, however, looked unconvinced. And Harwood's assurance began to waver when, hours later, Orneppu reappeared in company with Mervex and another of his kind, and boomed his solemn instructions.

"Listen, Earthlings! Soon we set sail for Drumgrade. During the first million miles or so, we must use the atomic engines. Therefore we must make precautionings so that you are not hurt by the shock of departing. Down on the floor, all of you!"

Intimidated by the glitter in the ever-changing lizard eyes, the grumbling prisoners had to obey. Just as when they were halted at the invisible wall in the spaceship, they seemed to be forced down to the floor by some outer compulsion.

Immediately their captors bent over them, lashing them down with silvery wire-like coils, which held them like leather thongs.

"Have no fear, Earthlings," soothed Orneppu. "This is only for a little while, until we have readified you for anti-time and anti-space."

Callahan's groan was loud and unrestrained. Eileen bit her underlip, trying in vain to keep back the tears. But Harwood's protest was fiercely indignant. "You thugs—you dirty thugs!" he swore.

None of his captors, however, seemed to hear him. In a businesslike way, the three of them finished binding the prisoners, then disappeared. At the same time, the victims felt a shuddering and jerking, as if the spaceship were being pulled to the surface of the sea. A long interval followed, during which the ship shook like a cork. Then there came a powerful jolt, and a whizzing sound. And the swaying and tossing of the ship gave place to a faint steady vibration.

It was not many minutes later when invisible hands began feeling at the prisoners' bodies, releasing their fastenings. Somewhat unsteadily, they flexed their cramped muscles, and rose to their feet.

But hardly had they regained their equilibrium when Eileen burst out hysterically, "Look! Heavens, just look!"

The quivering girl was pointing to a lozenge-shaped panel, covered with a transparent plastic, which had just opened in the vessel's otherwise unbroken walls.

Wide-eyed, the four gazed through the porthole. Above them—unblinking points of fire in a purple-black sky—they saw the stars. And beneath them, far beneath, mostly covered with cloud and shadow but with a bright crescent to the left like a much enlarged new moon, they observed an enormous globe.

"The Earth! The Earth!" they cried, and, overwhelmed, sank back upon the floor of the spaceship.

CHAPTER III

None of the travelers ever knew just when anti-space and anti-time were applied. All that they remembered was that a wide stretch of glowing purple wall was stripped away as by remote control, revealing a strange, complicated, red-plastic machine, with a multitude of knobs, sockets, and dials, perforations into which needle-like slits of metal were injected faster than the eye could follow, and crystalline, glass-like partitions wherein a swarm of indistinguishable shapes was moving as on a television screen when all is out of focus. A faint bluish mist surrounded the crystalline partitions, and a nauseating chemical odor was in the air.

Bewildered, the captives had started toward the machine, expecting to examine it more closely . . . when a blankness fell upon them. They reeled, they felt faint; then, before they could even cry out, they had plunged into insensibility.

It seemed only a moment later when they began to revive. Callahan groaned, and lifted himself to a sitting posture on the floor. Harwood, prone at the police chief's side, with the small black case still slung over his left shoulder, grumbled to himself, struggled to his feet, and offered a hand to Eileen, whom Ted was already helping up. At first no one noticed that the nauseating odor had disappeared.

But all were trying hard to collect their dazed senses.

"Just what—what struck us?" asked the girl, fighting to gain command of her tongue. "It was just like—well, like being hit with a club. My head—my head still hurts."

"It was some sort of anaesthetic—those gangsters drugged us," decided Harwood, who had been coughing again, and felt hot and feverish (and had not been helped much by some aspirins from a small box which Ted had happened to carry in one pocket).

He paused; passed one hand over his chin and cheeks, whose stubble had begun to grow during his captivity. "My beard doesn't seem any longer than before we were knocked out."

"Mine neither!" coincided Ted and Callahan.

Almost at the same time, Eileen made a more striking discovery. Having staggered over to the plastic-covered porthole, she gasped, threw one hand over her forehead, and tottered backward. Ted, fearing that she was about to faint, caught her in his arms. But she squirmed out of his clasp, and began pointing—pointing through the porthole with half-formed cries.

Callahan, the first of the men to reach the porthole, gave just a glance before the others had crowded him away—but one glance was enough. "Lord Almighty!" he muttered, his jaws falling wide apart.

Ted and Harwood, quickly taking turns at the porthole, joined the others in startled exclamations.

Directly opposite them through the porthole, at a distance of hundreds of thousands of miles, there was a luminous globe, of about the shape and color of an almost full moon, though with twenty times the full moon's radius. What most astonished the observers was not the globe's size but its specific features: the hand-shaped dark mass which, partly veiled in bands of cloud, occupied most of the central area of the disk; the three faintly shining round objects which, ranging in apparent size from that of a pea to that of a large grapefruit, surrounded the globe at various distances; and the dimly glowing belt, a little like the rings of Saturn, which encircled the planet at a distance of half a dozen diameters. On the globe's left rim there was a shadowy crescent, as in a moon not quite at its full.

"We're bewitched! Sure are bewitched!" mumbled Callahan, whose face had been drained of its normal ruddy glow.

"Just notice the stars!" broke in Ted, taking his second turn at the porthole, while Eileen peeped over his bent shoulders. "Those constellations—that one shaped just like a bottle—I've never seen them before!"

"And see! We're moving! Moving fast!" Eileen contributed, pointing excitedly. "That big bright world over there—don't you notice, we're getting nearer!"

"Oh, shucks, has everybody gone crazy?" growled Harwood. "Why, it can't be anything but an optical illusion!" However, he took another long glance—and became speechless.

But before anyone could express the amazing new

knowledge that had come to them all, they were aware of a shadowy intrusion—lizard shapes looming all around them, at first barely visible, then in vivid, ever-changing colors.

"Flat on the floor, all of you!" they heard a command in Mervex's squeaky voice.

"Now that we are free from anti-time and anti-space," Orneppu went on, "we are almost through with our voyaging. In one Earthling hour more, we will be on Drumgrade. Down on the floor, then! You must have protectionings from the landing jolts, which your soft bodies cannot bear!"

Once more, the prisoners had no choice but to obey. Once more, they were lashed down by silvery strands. Then, for a long time, they waited. They heard threshings and groans all about them, and scurryings and rattlings suggesting an unusual agitation. They caught sight of lizard forms flashing by with bright green, blue, or golden-yellow bodies and blinking tail-eyes.

"Oh, now what will they do with us?" Eileen echoed the thought in the minds of all.

"Nothing bad, I'm sure. Else they wouldn't take such pains to keep us alive," reasoned Ted. But his dearest wish was that one of his hands might be free to soothe the girl.

"Well, young man," answered Harwood, in a skeptical drawl, "maybe you're right. But don't forget that we on Earth take pains to preserve orang-utans headed for a zoo."

Callahan, meanwhile, was gritting his teeth; his thick, well-developed muscles strained mightily at his fetters. But the silvery cords held firm.

Then, even as he puffed and grew purple-faced,

there came a shattering noise, and a jolt that might have flung the passengers halfway through the spaceship had they not been tied. The whole vehicle shook and quivered. And as the vibrations gradually died down, the prisoners heard a confusion of sounds, and caught a whiff of perfumed air. At the same time, someone began feeling at their fastenings.

"Now you may get up, Earthlings!" Orneppu's deep voice roared in their ears. "Get up, all of you! We will introduce you to the queen of planets!"

CHAPTER IV

On both sides of the street, carrot-shaped towers and bubble-like domes projected, each dominated by a long spear-pointed spire. The edifices were of various pale tints, from faintest blue, pink, and violet to a diluted glimmery golden and milky white. All had the shimmery quality of mother-of-pearl, and all curved into their neighbors so gracefully that they seemed merged in a unified whole. Through fan-shaped and crescent apertures dotting the buildings, pale green and purplish lights flickered, and purplish banners streamed from the roofs.

All were bathed in the light of a yellow-white sun, somewhat smaller than the sun of Earth but slightly more brilliant; in two hours, it had risen twenty degrees above the western horizon. Three widely scattered pallid moons of various sizes, shone in the deep-blue sky.

The street, broad as a boulevard, curved like a country lane. On each side stretched a transparent plastic wall nearly twelve feet high, and behind the walls a multitude stared—creatures shadowy thin, or colored ruby red, lemon yellow, orange, emerald, or indigo. All were lizard-shaped, some taller than the tallest man, others of the size of tiny children; and all had long flat tails with eyes that glittered and sparkled, wedge-shaped heads each with two pairs of eyes, and waving octopus-like tentacles. A variety of sounds, from squeals of excitement to low rumblings, came from them incessantly.

As they milled about, their seven-clawed hands pointed to the center of the street, where a platform about ten feet wide moved with a low whirring at the speed of a rapidly walking man. From the wildly threshing throng, a howl went up as a procession of tall structures approached around a curve of the street, dominated by a crystalline edifice as tall as a two-story house. Here, on a throne-like seat, a lizard-shaped dignitary perched motionless, while, on a slightly lower platform to his rear, others of his kind sat around a red-wired cage-like container.

Pandemonium now filled the air—shrieks of amazement, wonder, horror, and disgust, while the observers pressed close to the glass partition.

Within the red-wired container stood four unlizard-like tailless creatures, all of them staring at the mob with quite as much interest as the mob showed in them. They were pale from the shock of disembarkation at dawn, they could not even conjecture their approaching fate, yet they felt some of the excitement of travelers in a strange new country. Some things, at least, were in their favor. The air of Drumgrade was rich in oxygen. Its sun was bright and life-giving; the temperature was high, but no more so than on a warm summer's day on Earth. To their joy, they found that they were lighter and could move a little more freely than on Earth, showing that the hold of gravity was slightly less than they had known.

"Oh, I'm sure everything will be all right!" Eileen exclaimed, tring to hold up her courage. "I just *know* everything will be all right!"

Harwood, struggling with his cold, coughed his dissent. "Well, young lady," he rasped, "if you think it's all right being kidnapped and carried God knows how many trillions of miles from home—"

He was interrupted by the deep bass of Orneppu, who had never left them since their disembarkation.

"Now, Earthlings, is not a time for disputings. I have much to tell you of your new environings."

"Where on Earth are we now—I mean, where in heaven?" asked Ted, as they turned a sharp curve and passed a park filled with yellow-green fernlike trees more than a hundred feet high.

"We are in the city Arvandu, the second most large in our great world-nation Sarvun," Mervex hastened to explain.

As they passed the intersection of a side-street, Eileen pressed close to Ted with a gasp of horror, pointing to several six-legged and four-eyed animals of about the size and shape of large crocodiles, which were rambling about like dogs.

"Arvandu," Orneppu went on, "is the home of Olero, our most great Trivate or ruler of the province of Ranvan. We are on our way to see him. It is his desiring to be showed all the specimens from other planets. He will make the deciding what to do with you."

A stunned silence ensued, during which Ted and Eileen tried to look hopeful, Harwood groaned, and

Callahan flexed and unflexed his thick right arm as if for instant action.

"What are all these—these ghastly crowds doing on the street?" the detective demanded. "Why, they're staring just as if we're circus animals!"

"Then you think it happens every day," answered Orneppu, impatiently, "that they see monsters from another world?"

"Well, at any rate," remarked Ted, pointing to the plastic partitions that fenced off the crowd, "we're protected from their getting too close to us."

"Those walls," snorted Orneppu, contemptuously, "are not to protection *you* from them. They are to protection *them* from you!"

"You see how it is," Harwood remarked to his companions. "Just the way we'd feel about chumming with boa constrictors."

As they learned more about the Trivate Olero, none of them were reassured.

"He is the only Trivate in all Ranvan," Orneppu rumbled on. "Trivate is a very hard word to translation. It means—well, the great Thought Distributing Center."

"Thought Distributing Center?" asked Ted. "Ah, I think I understand. He sends out orders, messages, reports—he's a sort of propaganda boss."

"No, he is not!"

There was a moment's pause, while the platform whirred on past a square filled with many-colored fountains and statues of immense long-tailed and tentacled five-eyed lizards.

"He works," continued Orneppu, "by sending out thoughts, which are picked up by the under-officials."

"You mean, it's what we call thought transference —mind reading—mental telepathy? Olero is a great psychic?"

"No, he is not!"

This denial was followed by an impatient snort.

"Olero's powers, they are not like your thought transference. His powers are electric, like your radio. They come from rays which he sends into the air. All Drumgradians have electric organs to send and receive messagings, but the Olero's organs are more—well, more keen than most. You see these tentacles coming out of my face?"

Ted grunted an affirmative. He had often wondered as to the purpose of the tentacles.

"They are part of our messaging tools, though part also grow inside our heads. You remember that, in the spaceship *Great Galaxy,* you could not walk more than a little distance. That was because our organs, they sent out electric waves that would not let you pass."

While this conversation was occurring, they entered a new district. Instead of the carrot-shaped towers and bubble-like palaces, there were only blank gray tentlike hovels whose sides flapped loosely on bare rocky hills, while the steep slopes were leveled as by a gigantic plane above tall piles of boulders and rubble. No fountain played here, no trees raised their fernlike foliage, but lusterless lizard shapes scurried about like roaches and disappeared into some of the many round dark holes in the tentlike structures and in the rock walls. A peculiar fetid odor, as of decaying vegetables, filled the entire region.

"Do not attention this place," advised Orneppu. "We will soon be out of it. It is what we call the Narg, where our most worthless people live—that is, those who own very little or nothing. Now let us turn back to Olero."

"Are you telling us," asked Callahan, "he sends his thoughts out through empty space?"

"Space, she is not empty. She is full of rays and vibrationings. Olero's organs are very keen. He sends his will more than a hundred of your Earthling miles. He uses vibrationings outside your Earthling range. Thus he sends out the laws which he makes."

"You don't mean to say," broke in Harwood, "anything he says is law?"

"Yes, anything he says is law. It is a most beautiful system. It makes it so simple to govern."

"Then he could sentence a man to death—and with no appeal?"

Orneppu gave his tail a quick annoyed thump.

"Why not—if he had a reason? But have no fear, Earthlings. He would not harm anyone unless for the good of Arvandu."

The four strangers, as the moving platform bore them through a rock wall into a district of graceful domed dwellings surrounded by clumps of twelve-foot grass and scarlet flowers as large as a man's head, were less eager than ever to meet the ruler.

Meanwhile, with a low whirring, the platform passed through the gates in two farther walls, the first of which was composed of sword-like leaves that drew back as the party approached. Then they wound to a halt before a tall, moat-guarded barricade of a glassy bottle-green plastic.

Orneppu, who had been visible all during the trip through the city, dismounted from the platform. From the edges of his tentacles, reddish sparks were flashing in a rhythmic succession, while he stood stockstill, almost erect on his two legs, like a man listening intently to a telephone conversation.

"Olero says," announced Orneppu, as the sparks suddenly ceased, "that we must go in at once."

Instantly, like a theater curtain pulled by invisible strings, the plastic barricade drew apart. But all that the visitors saw was a purple mist, through which, at a word from Orneppu, they proceeded on foot, while Mervex, at one side, prodded them on like a mule-driver. It seemed that they walked a long distance before suddenly the mist disappeared, unbaring an immense chamber, its vaulted purple roof as high as that of a great cathedral, its curving walls shimmering with rainbow tints, which shed a pale though sufficient illumination.

On a long raised satiny purple couch in the center of the great hall, a green-scaled figure was reclining amid a score of variously colored attendants. His lizard form was exceptionally large—fully ten feet from head to tip of tail. His head was of disproportionate size, and his two front eyes, marked by enormous black pupils, glowed with an orange brilliance, while his rear eyes flickered with an ominous-looking copper and his tail-eye blinked blue and red. His most astonishing features, however, were his tentacles, which were longer than a man's arm, and were constantly squirming like snakes, while a succession of sparks scintillated from their ends in fascinating but terrifying colors—crimson, violet, parsley green, white, dandelion yellow, vermilion, and deep purple.

As Orneppu and Mervex and several of their fellows drew near with the visitors from Earth, the Trivate's attendants made way for their approach amid squeaks, squeals, and gasps, and stretched their tails flat along the floor in token of homage. Several of them, however, took their places with great composure at various points about the hall, and pulled out little parchment-like rolls, set them up on small stands, and began marking them with long, straight instruments that were like crosses between brushes and pens. Not until later did the Earth-folk realize that artists were sketching them.

Meanwhile, they had approached within a few feet of His Highness, who examined them in silence for a long while, first with his orange front eyes, then with his coppery rear eyes, then with his blinking tail-eye, though this required him to swing about in a half circle. After a time, he turned to Orneppu, who stood a few feet in front of him, bending far forward on his big front legs, his clawed hands stretched out in an attitude of respect, if not of reverence.

Then, from the tips of Olero's long tentacles, the many-colored sparks began to flash more vividly than ever, and after a time were followed by a similar but briefer series from Orneppu's tentacles, which in turn were succeeded by further sparks from the Trivate. Even though no sound could be heard, the observers knew that a conversation was taking place.

At last Orneppu swung toward the prisoners, who had been standing anxiously at one side. "Our great leader Olero," he informed them, "wishes to make some questionings."

The hearts of all four sank.

"I will translation everything for our noble Trivate," Orneppu continued. "You there"—he designated Ted with a flick of one seven-fingered hand—"you answer the questionings."

"I'll try my best."

"Our lord Olero," the interpreter went on, "says that you give him much puzzling. I should tell you that we chosed your planet Earth because its conditions were more like Drumgrade's than we could find on any other world. That being so, Olero says you Earthlings should be like us Drumgradians—strong and beautiful, and not weak, scaleless, tailless monsters. The Trivate asks to know how you can get along half blind."

"We're not half blind!"

"Oh, yes, you are! More than half blind! You have eyes only in front. You cannot see behind you at all. Worst of all, you have no tail-eye."

"That doesn't make us half blind—" Ted protested. But Orneppu, paying no attention, was exchanging another series of tentacle flashes with the Trivate.

"Also," the interpreter resumed, "Olero wants to know how can you walk without a tail to make a balancing for your weight. How can you get along without tentacles to send and receive your messagings? How can you work with half hands?"

"Half hands?"

"Well, you have only five fingers, and these have no claws. Again—" Orneppu paused to designate Ted's luxuriant black hair and his face stubbled with several days' growth of beard—"the Trivate asks what those strings are on your head. And those ugly wrappings around your body."

"Those are my clothes! Didn't you see, Orneppu, that everybody on Earth wore them? We need them to protect us from the cold, and for looks and decency."

Again there was a series of sparks between Orneppu

and the Trivate. The four visitors meanwhile exchanged worried glances.

"Olero says," the interpreter confided, after a time, "why can't you grow scales? They are comfortable, they look good, they are decent, they are all the protectionings we need in a warm climate like Drumgrade's. When we—what do you say?—outgrow them, all we do is shed them and grow another set."

Next Orneppu mentioned the captives' teeth, which, he said, were like the weapons of certain of the Drumgradian lower animals. But the people needed no such primitive aids, since all their food was soft and synthetic, and required no chewing.

"Now, by gum, I see why you all have mouths like my old grandad," Callahan contributed. But no one seemed to notice this remark as Orneppu went on, with one clawed hand pointed at Eileen.

"Here, Earthlings, is what makes the most puzzling for Olero. There are two kinds of you. Three of you are of one species, and the other has a different body, more rounded, and not so ugly. The Trivate thinks this one belongs to a different species. Having been on Earth, I know this is not so. But the Trivate—he asks for your explainings."

Ted hesitated, embarrassed. Harwood, whose cold was troubling him more than ever, was unable to restrain a violent fit of coughing, which brought a glare of surprise and indignation to the Trivate's orange front eyes. The attendants stared at the detective in a startled way, as if they had never heard coughing before. But the artists, at various points in the hall, continued vigorously sketching.

"Well," Ted answered Olero's last question, "ask your leader—has he never heard of sex?"

There was another interchange of sparks between the interpreter and the ruler.

"Naturally. But he still has great puzzling. People of different sexes on Drumgrade—they look so much alike you cannot tell them apart. Besides, the Trivate wishes to know if you permit sex to all. Surely, not everyone is allowed to have young ones."

"Of course—everyone who is physically able."

Further sparks, marked by bright reds and flaring yellows, lasted for a long while before Orneppu again addressed Ted.

"The Trivate, he cannot understand. How, then, can you regulation your population?"

"Well, how do *you* regulate your population?"

"That is not hard, Earthling. Five out of every hundred are chosed to give us all the males and females we need. These produce just the number of offspring the Trivate sets, which need not be many, since we live ten times more long than you Earthlings. How could we keep from having too much population if everyone was allowed to have young ones?"

"But what," demanded Ted, "of the ninety-five per cent of your people who do not reproduce?"

"Oh, for them we have harmless sterilizing. They make our most leading people, the Neuters. I myself—I am proud to be one, and so is the Trivate. The Neuters, not being used up by child-bearing and child-raising, do our most important work."

While Ted was trying to absorb this information, Mervex's long claws had reached out, lifted the spectacles from his eyes, and passed them to Olero, who had evidently never seen their like. But the ruler's puzzled frown, as he returned the articles, showed that he had not been enlightened by examining them. "He wants to know," inquired Orneppu, "if you have to wear them to make up for the eyes which you do not have."

Before Ted could reply, a more brilliant series of sparks than ever issued from the Trivate's long weaving tentacles.

"At last he has decisioned what to do with you," stated Orneppu, when the sparks had ended. And the slow, ominous rumble in his voice came to the hearers' ears like a warning blast.

CHAPTER V

"This way, Earthlings!"

Orneppu, with Mervex following, started off from the Trivate's side, while three of his kind joined him. Flashing from invisibility to sapphire-blue or sea-green, they moved lithely on their long legs, and led the captives into a court where palm-trees with fronds as wide as a house rose to the height of redwood trees. Ted and Eileen would have paused to examine the scarlet and golden parrot-shaped birds, which sang like larks, but the guides, with threatening claws, hurried them on through long purple-lined corridors.

At last they halted in an immense hall lighted with a hard blue radiance. Shining plastic bands and panels, slowly rotating dark metallic wheels, meshes of coppery wire that reached from the high ceiling in intricate patterns like gigantic cobwebs, and scores of tall funnel-shaped projections on the floor, drew the strangers' attention, while their nostrils recoiled from a combination of acrid chemical odors.

"By jiminy, a laboratory, unless I miss my guess!" decided Ted, excitedly.

"And unless I miss *my* guess," Harwood added, glumly, between sniffs and sneezes, "it's nothing for our good!"

"She is what we call the Xoltek—or, as nearly as I can say it in your language, the Tabulating Center," rumbled Orneppu. "We have brought you here for some testings."

"Let's pray it won't be the way we test white rats and guinea pigs," muttered Harwood, whose pessimism seemed justified an instant later, when Orneppu ordered, "Down on the floor, all of you!"

As in the spaceship, the prisoners were bound with silvery cords, while devices resembling electrodes were fastened to their foreheads and throats. Tears of pain and indignation sparkled in Eileen's eyes. Harwood and Callahan mumbled curses, while Ted, as he struggled with the cords, tried to reassure Eileen with hopes that he did not really feel. "In just a few minutes," he predicted, "we'll all be free again—"

"Oh, God, look at that!" screamed the girl.

Down from the ceiling, strange instruments were swinging on metallic ropes: telescope-shaped tubes made of many strands of wire in concentric circles; and tinny-looking football-sized objects, which throbbed like motors. But most alarming was the enormous apparatus containing three large rings, which glared with patches of deep-blue, orange, emerald, and incandescent white against a yellowish background. On its base, as it descended in a wide ellipse, there was a head-sized transparent ball of scarlet, from which a dazzling red beam was pointed with such intensity that the watchers had to close their eyes when it was briefly focussed on each of them successively.

Meanwhile, they heard queer grunts and murmurings from the Drumgradians, who, as soon as the scarlet light had faded, rushed to a wall panel, from which a gray plastic tape, covered with small perforations, was issuing like toothpaste from a tube. With staring front and rear eyes, the Drumgradians examined the perforations for several minutes; then, with squeaks and squeals of surprise, they turned back to their captives and cut their cords.

"So! Didn't I tell you it would be all right?" Ted asked, as he helped Eileen back to her feet.

"It is more than all right. I congratulation you, Earthling!" boomed Orneppu, as he pointed seven clawed fingers at Ted. "I congratulation you for being the chosen one!"

Why was it that Ted's heart gave a leap of fear?

"I congratulation you because you have been chosen by our testing machine, which can judge everything in you with one flash of light. It has ranked you first of all the Earthlings."

"First—in what way?"

"First in what we call *chelgruk*—which may be translationed as your power to serve Drumgrade. Now come with me!"

Ted, having noticed the other men's dismay and Eileen's shocked look, drew back abruptly.

"Oh, Ted, Ted dear—you can't—it's monstrous! You can't leave me here!" cried the girl, flinging herself toward him. "What under heaven will ever become of me now?"

"Don't worry! I'll never abandon you!" he tried to console her, while she clung to him. Combatively he drew himself up to his full five feet eleven, and turned back to Orneppu, whose tail, swinging menacingly, was giving out green and ruby-red sparks from its blinking eye.

"I'll not be coming with you!" he proclaimed.

A grating laughter sounded from Orneppu.

"What is that, Earthling? You think that's for you to say?"

His tail lashed out, and a sharp pain stabbed at Ted's left leg. In the same tormented instant, he saw three lizard forms surrounding him, and read the implacable commands in the vari-colored glaring eyes.

"What do you intend doing with me?"

"At the proper time, Earthling, you will find out!"

"But my friends—what of my friends?" With a sweeping gesture, Ted indicated the three other captives. "What are you going to do with them?"

"That, too, you will find out!"

Eileen, wrenched from Ted by a seven-clawed arm, shrieked, and tried to force her way back to him. But an infant might as well have fought a grown man.

Callahan, nevertheless, pressed forward to the rescue. But he was brushed lightly aside, and was left as if tied to one spot, uselessly shaking his fist, and growling oaths.

Harwood, looking on dourly, seemed to realize the futility of resistance as Ted, still hotly protesting, was led toward the U-shaped opening in the floor between two shadowy, long-tailed forms. Mervex, however, remained behind.

For a long while, having descended a stone stairway, Ted wound with his guides through long curved and sloping galleries, dimly lit with a purplish glow from the walls. "Where are we going?" he demanded of Orneppu, whom he recognized as one of his escorts. But the only answer was an abrupt, "Through the

Ruzz—which may be translationed as the Undershoots—underground passagings—the quickest way between buildings."

He was relieved when at last they halted before a large five-sided door, which swung open automatically, revealing a moderate-sized room with a nave-like ceiling and slightly concave walls lighted with the usual purple glow. There were no windows, and the bare stone floor held no furniture.

"Here, Earthling, we have made every provisioning for you. The Trivate commands you to stay here," announced Orneppu, as he shepherded Ted into the room.

Feeling like a man who has just heard himself sentenced for life to a dungeon, Ted groaned, and at first could say nothing. What provision could be made for him in this bare box?

Orneppu, as if reading the expression on his face, stepped on a small floor panel, and a three-legged table leapt out of the wall. He stepped on another panel, and a stool and a bench sprang forth. He stepped on a third, and a low couch-like contrivance made its appearance. A small enclosure with washing and bathing facilities followed, along with several brown loaf-shaped objects such as the Earth-people had been eating ever since their kidnapping. And this was supplemented by coppery vessels containing a clear, tasteless fluid with the properties of both food and drink.

"Our noble Trivate," Orneppu explained, "has ordered that you remain here until you learn our language. I myself will instruction you, so that you may talk soon with our specializers, who wish to solve the mysteries of Earthling life."

"But I supposed," protested Ted, "that you spoke mostly by thought transference—sparks and flashes of light—"

"That is true among our high officials. Usually the people, and sometimes our leaders also in not so important doings, use the crude older speech-making voice."

Ted was pacing back and forth like a fox in a cage. His long arms swung excitedly; his eyes were black fires in his long, mobile face.

"You see," Orneppu went on, in his usual sonorous tones, as he pointed to the many little perforations on a small patch in the wall, "we have automatic ventilationing. That switch over there is for the intaking and outgoing air. That switch above it is for the temperature—"

"But, Lord, I need more than air and temperature control!" Ted paused in his floor pacing long enough to rap angrily at the wall. "What, too, of my friends? Are we to remain separated? Won't I even know what's happened to them? Are they also being locked up?"

Orneppu grunted something in his own language, and his tentacles waved with worm-like wrigglings. His tail thumped against the floor. "I can tell you only what Olero allows," he answered, enigmatically. "But I can give you this messaging. Nothing will happen to the other Earthlings except what is for the best of Drumgrade. Now come! We waste time!"

He pressed another floor panel, and there came a rattling, clattering, and clanging as a sort of wired box of about the size of a stall shower shot out of a hidden wall compartment. Ted saw that it contained a miscellany of small springs, wheels, and metal rods, which reminded him of clockwork.

"I know that you Earthlings must have exercising. So you may operation this machine. Step into it!"

Having no idea what lay in store, Ted entered through a door on one side of the wired box. Instantly something beneath him whirred and began leaping swiftly up and down. Ted, lest he be caught and mangled, had no choice but to move his legs in time, at the speed of a sprinter in a hundred-yard dash. In a minute or two, he was almost exhausted, and was wondering desperately how to end the unwanted workout when he saw that Orneppu was pointing to a little red panel to his left, which he pushed with one hand, halting the machine.

"Whew!" Ted reflected, as he came out panting. "I've never worked so hard before just to stay in one place."

"That is our Gillyco, or what you would call an Exercising Machine," explained Orneppu. "It is used by most busy Drumgradians, for of course they have no time for out-of-date exercising like running and walking."

Ted mumbled something to himself, foreseeing that he would not overuse the Gillyco.

"Now when I am away," the instructor went on, "there will be many things for you to do. Here, I will show you!"

He opened another wall panel, and drew forth some thin pale-gray sheets of metal and several slender plastic rods, whose points glistened as if tipped with diamonds. The sharp points, Orneppu demonstrated, made scratches on the metal, and the scratches—

which could be erased with an acid, until the metal wore too thin—constituted the native writing.

"I will show you how to write. Then, when I am away, you will make practice!" said Orneppu, as he made notations in wavy lines diagonally from right to left across one of the sheets.

He pressed another panel, and, with a rustling, a silvery screen unrolled from the ceiling and covered an entire wall. Across this screen, life-sized figures flashed as in color television, but not quite as in television; they seemed three-dimensional, and the impression of many-hued, long-tailed lizards was so real that Ted shrank back as from the actual beasts.

"By listening when I am gone," stated his teacher, "you will instruction yourself about our language. Now, Earthling, I go!"

There came a low thudding and grating, and Orneppu had disappeared. As the heavy door clanged to a close and he found himself alone in the big, empty, silent room, Ted experienced a sense of claustrophobia. But his thoughts were less on his own fate than on Eileen's, though he felt as helpless as a caged rat to aid her or any of the captives.

"Oh, what will they do to him now? When, when will I ever see him again?" wailed Eileen, weeping convulsively as Ted disappeared through the U-shaped opening in the floor.

Dismayed and hesitant, Callahan and Harwood stood over her.

"Come, come, Miss, what's the need to carry on like that?" The police chief tried to pacify her, while automatically flexing and unflexing the muscles of his big right arm to keep up his own courage. "Don't you worry, we'll take care of you!"

"Listen, my girl!" Harwood added. "I've had reams of experience. I know that just when the mesh seems to be most tangled it's often the nearest to unraveling. Believe me, I've cracked harder cases than this!"

Trying her best to check her sobs, Eileen wept on and on.

Even Mervex, who stood hovering near in shadowy outlines, seemed uncertain what to do. But his spasmodic tail-sparkles showed his irritation.

"Quit that noise!" he finally commanded, in incisive squeaks. "Never in all my days—and I have lived more than a hundred thousand of them—have I heard anything so foolish. Not even our infants make such a commotioning. Quit it at once!"

The only effect was to make Eileen weep the more.

"If you keep up this racket," shrilled Mervex, "you will not be of any use for the purposing showed here in the Xoltek."

He strode uneasily about the hall, faded out of sight, and flashed back in a brilliant yellow. His tail was swaying like an aroused cat's.

"Listen!" he burst out, in tones that drilled their way through the listeners. "The machine has found that you"—he pointed at Eileen with one projecting claw—"have much *chelgruk*. You are the most gentle of all the Earthlings. The others—they all have bad tempers, like—well, what do you call them?—wild animals. But you—the machine shows that you would make some young Drumgradians an amusing plaything."

Eileen's lips drew wide apart in a new fear as she looked up with a tear-stained face. "What's that?"

"Did you not hear me? The machine says you would make young Drumgradians a good plaything."

"Plaything?" Incredulously she shrank back, with eyes distended. "You mean—a pet?"

"Well, whatever you Earthlings would call it, have no fear. You will be most well cared for, in a nest of your own. You will be given only to the most high-born childs—"

Mervex hesitated, not quite sure of the word.

"Children," Harwood supplied.

"High-born children. Wait, I will send for some!"

From the ends of his tentacles, a rhythmic series of blue and red sparks flashed. A long time went by, while Eileen dabbed at her swollen eyes, dried her tears, and tried to look brave. The two men, turning to her with occasional soothing words, were slowly pacing back and forth among the tall funnel-shaped floor projections, while the dark metallic wheels rotated above them and the meshes of coppery wire, stretching down from the ceiling, looked more than ever like colossal cobwebs.

"Well, Callahan," the detective muttered glumly to his companion between coughs, while his small greenish eyes stared at the silvery walls as if trying to pierce them, "I hope these monsters don't try to make household toys of us too—"

"Sure, old man, you don't need to be afraid," answered the police chief, his strained face widening in an attempt at jocularity. He mopped at a watery nose, for he had caught Harwood's cold. "A swell pet you'd make, with a leather collar round your neck, and maybe a license tag hanging down in front, and a harness and chain—"

"And you'd look just lovely, Chief, in a doghouse,"

Harwood retorted, with a wry attempt at a smile. "Why, they might even throw you a bone now and then, and let you shake paws if you were good, and teach you lots of cute tricks—"

They were interrupted by a sudden din as a pear-shaped partition in the wall turned inward, admitting five young Drumgradians, of about the size of Earthly ten-year-olds. Their tails waved excitedly, with colored eye-flashes; their half-developed tentacles twisted and squirmed; their seven-clawed hands reached out eagerly; their colors changed from bright red to flaring yellow; piercing squeaks and screams came from the purplish jaws that slit their toothless wedge-shaped heads. When they saw the Earth-folk, they let out even shriller cries, doubled over, and rocked in laughter.

Instantly Mervex, uttering a few sharp, decisive sounds in Drumgradian, turned toward Eileen—at which the eager young crowd surrounded her, shrieking in ever wilder glee, and pointing to her hair, her teeth, her fingers, her dress, her shoes with spasms of mirth. One daring young hopeful jabbed at her arm as if to make sure that it was real. And as she winced from the pain, another tormentor pulled at her red locks, and a third nipped her leg with seven sharp claws.

Callahan, at the same time, was starting forward in an effort to save the girl. His fist was about to come down when, as many times before, he was stopped as by an invisible wall.

"The devils!" he growled. "The dirty devils! If I only had my good old automatic—"

Eileen, in the midst of the young Drumgradians, was being forced toward the pear-shaped door. Vainly struggling, she disappeared. The shouts and shrieks of her oppressors still sounded in the men's ears as the partition slid back and they confronted one another with blank, hopeless faces.

But before they had had time to speak, Mervex and another Drumgradian began pointing toward the U-shaped floor opening in which Ted had vanished sometime before.

"Over there, Earthlings!"

"What are you going to do with us?" Harwood snapped.

"Only as the machine directions us. But this I can say: we will make use of your *chelgruk*—your power to serve Drumgrade."

If either man at that moment had been able to blow Drumgrade to dust, the planet would not have survived another instant. But actually all that they could do was to go dragging between two lizard forms through the U-shaped opening.

Counting their footsteps, Harwood estimated that they wound at least a mile through the purplish galleries before halting in a hall even larger than the Tabulation Center. Octagonal, and with a domed ceiling, it was walled and roofed with a translucent pearly plastic through which a subdued sunlight penetrated, though the observers could make out no object outside. There were no windows, and the pearly material was held in place by a symmetrical branching network of a pale, aluminum-like alloy.

"Phew! Smells like formaldehyde!" diagnosed Harwood, sniffing disapprovingly.

The disagreeable odor was almost overpowering. But what chiefly held the men's attention were the scores of low tables, before which scores of lizard shapes crouched, supported on their long legs and long, thick tails. From the tentacles of them all, thin tubes and wires stretched to the objects on the table, which the newcomers identified as small living creatures: lizard-like reptiles, parrot-like birds such as they had seen in the palm-grove, and a round-bodied, slimy ball of an animal that moved by rolling itself slowly along. Here and there a tiny dismembered scaly body lay. In red-wired cages against the wall, beasts like tentacled rats flitted and squeaked and snaky monsters with javelin-pointed tails writhed and squirmed.

"Lordy!" exclaimed Callahan. "So they're taking us to the zoo?"

"Looks more to me like an experimental laboratory," Harwood decided. "We'll be damned lucky if we're not material for the experiments."

He had hardly spoken when invisible arms seized him and his companion and lashed them to two adjoining tables. Their struggles were useless; within a minute, they were both bound so tightly that they could move neither an arm nor a leg.

"Have no fear, Earthlings," came the squeaky tones of Mervex. "Have no fear. We use only the most perfectioned techniques. You will feel no pain."

The prisoners, in desperate attempts at relief, gasped and jerked their heads slightly. They were finding it hard to breathe.

A muffled shriek from just to the left, where a scaly cat-shaped object lay tied, did nothing to reassure them.

"Now, Earthlings, quiet! Quiet!" Mervex directed, a little in the way of a dentist counseling a child not to fear the drill. "That will make everything more easy.

Remember, it all will be for the good of Drumgrade and the noble purposings of science, which must investigation your reactings so as to compare you with our native animals."

Callahan groaned, and Harwood glared, but neither was able to speak. With a swoop of one seven-clawed hand, a shadowy form had seized the little black box slung over the detective's left shoulder.

"What is that?" Mervex demanded, his lizard jaws wide apart with a puzzled look; and he loosened Harwood's bindings sufficiently to permit him to speak.

Harwood coughed; hesitated. "That," he stated, with a wily glint in his eyes, "is what we on Earth call a good-luck prize—a charm to keep off bad spirits."

Mervex let out a disgusted grunt, gave a final glance at the black box, returned it to its owner, and muttered something about the folly of Earthlings.

Neither victim could ever recall all the details of the ordeal that followed. Both, however, had hazy recollections of shadowy beings standing over them like nightmare monsters, with long narrow tubes attached to their tentacles. They recalled blazing scarlet lights that flashed into their eyes, and electrical shocks that gripped their limbs in excruciating agonies. They had an impression of darting needle-like implements that penetrated their flesh, and of foul vapors pressed against their nostrils in sponge-like little wads. They knew that their mouths were pried open and small portions of their teeth sawed off, and that cuttings were taken from their nails and hair. They suspected that the implements moving constantly over their bodies were recording blood pressure, heartbeat, and temperature on the clocklike dials of small wall machines, of which they had caught glimpses. They were certain that the rods which dug into their ankles, and emerged with splashes of a rich red, were taking blood specimens. Meanwhile their constant silent prayer was that the long ordeal would end, end very soon.

But only after a long time, when a spearlike object as thick as a lead pencil was plunged into their legs, did they find relief. All at once they blacked out; and it may have been hours later when they awoke, to find that they were no longer in the great octagonal hall. Callahan, the first of the pair to come to himself, drew a calloused hand over his aching forehead, and stared in perplexity across a small windowless purple-lighted room. Dimly he made out a couch-like object, where the long, slender form of Harwood was stretched out a few feet away.

"Lord be praised!" he muttered, stirring slightly and finding that there were no longer any cords around his arms and legs. "I sure thought we'd never come through this alive!"

Harwood opened his eyes in a bewildered way.

"I—I don't feel exactly alive," he grumbled, after a minute. "I—I feel like I've waked up in hell."

"We've been drugged, old man," concluded Callahan. "It's just like somebody's dropped a ton of lead on my head."

"My—my teeth—front one aches like the devil," muttered Harwood with a wry grimace. "The fiends cut off a piece." Dismally he displayed a gap in an upper incisor.

"You didn't have my luck, old man," answered Callahan, becoming almost cheerful as he pointed to his own mouth. "See here! Those idiots took a slice off an old false tooth!"

A shrill voice from the invisible cut short the discussion.

"You Earthlings have no power of resisting. We Drumgradians—we would not have been put to sleep by the harmless little drug we injectioned to test your reactings. Now we must waste time until you recover and we can go on with the testing."

"Go on with what testing?"

"The same testing, Earthlings. We still have not learned one tenth enough for our science."

The prisoners heard a sudden grating sound, and caught a glimpse of a long-tailed shadowy form as it vanished through an 8-shaped door, which clanged to a close behind it.

"The demons!" growled Harwood.

"What are we going to do about it, old fellow?"

"Well, as soon as these fumes clear up in my head, I'll have to think. There must be some way. Two intelligent humans, surely, can outwit a lot of crazy overgrown lizards. I'll have to think, Callahan. There must be some way."

CHAPTER VI

"Well, George old man, what do you make of it now?"

"Gets to be more and more of a riddle, Chief. Either those blamed lizards have all gone crazy, or they've got some infernal new plot brewing."

Glumly Harwood and Callahan stared about their small purple-lighted room, and for a moment neither spoke. The detective's headache and toothache had long ago disappeared. Three days, according to Harwood's self-winding watch, had passed since they had first awakened in this prison; and during that time strange things had been happening. For the first thirty-six hours, they had been attended regularly by Mervex, and had been provided with water and their usual food and drink, which, though unpalatable, had nourished them well enough. But during the past thirty-six hours, no attendant had appeared, and the captives had been getting hungry and thirsty. The ventilating system, which had kept them well supplied with fresh air, had evidently broken down; the atmosphere was becoming stifling.

"What in hell has happened?" Callahan kept asking. "Maybe it's all part of a plot to starve or suffocate us."

Harwood meanwhile, with painstaking precision, had been testing every square inch of the walls, floor, and ceiling of their little enclosure. No sign of any door or window was visible, although Mervex had come in through a little five-sided opening, which had automatically appeared and disappeared upon his coming and going.

"Never can tell, Chief, maybe there's some secret lock or catch," the detective kept muttering, though Callahan would merely grunt in reply, "Even if there is, old man, think those blasted lizards are going to let us just walk out?"

Nevertheless, toward the end of the third day, Harwood's persistency was rewarded; his exploring fingers discovered a little metal ring, no larger than the nail of his small finger, which he had hitherto missed because it was concealed beneath a fluffy substance high up amid the ventilation holes just below the ceiling. Without understanding what he was doing, he jerked the ring—and instantly there came a whizzing and a whirring, and a five-sided opening stared at them from the wall.

"Quick! Before it closes again!" cried Harwood.

Followed by the police chief, he had just slipped through when, with a nerve-racking jar and rattling, the opening closed behind them.

"Lord! Now we're locked out! Can't get back even if we want to!" pointed Callahan, with the feeling of an animal suddenly barred from its cage.

They found themselves to be in a corridor of about a man's height, and barely wide enough to accommodate the two of them side by side. It was rectangular in shape except for the slanting ceiling; it was lighted with the usual purplish glow; and it curved to the left, making it impossible to see more than about fifty yards ahead. But the air was better than in the cell, and the two men took long relieved breaths.

"Well now, maybe our luck's changing—" Callahan had started to say, when Harwood silenced him by putting one hand to his lips.

"Never can tell who's listening, Chief," he whispered. Then cautiously, foot by foot, with Callahan just at his heels, he began making his way down the corridor. Though neither man had any idea where they were going, both accepted Callahan's philosophical view, "Sure, no matter what happens, we ain't got a deuced lot to lose."

After crawling several hundred yards, they received their first shock. At a point where the gallery widened to receive a small tributary corridor, Harwood started back with a gasp; his normally pale features went several degrees whiter. Callahan, almost colliding with him in his eagerness, also gasped and halted.

Before them on the stone pavement, a lizard was lying, his tail stretched out behind him. His seven-clawed arms squirmed convulsively. His five eyes had lost their glow. His tentacles were swollen, and exuded a disgusting slime. In a pained, listless way, he looked up at the two men; and then, suddenly and sharply, he sneezed. Immediately his sneeze was followed by a cough—a deep, racking cough, as of an asthmatic victim.

They had hardly had time to discuss this incident when, at another intersection, they observed two more Drumgradians, both flat on their backs, sneezing and coughing. A little farther on, they saw three others in the same condition, none of whom threw the men more than brief, dull glances.

"You know what?" decided Harwood, after they had passed the third group. "They've all caught my cold!"

"But it's worse than any cold—"

"Seems that way, but that doesn't prove a thing. Probably colds were never known on this planet before, and the natives haven't built up any immunity. It's just as when measles and other white men's diseases wiped out whole primitive tribes."

"So you think this'll wipe the lizards out?"

"I didn't say that. But it might, possibly. At any rate, it's knocked them out for the time—which explains why Mervex quit coming to our cell, and left us without food, drink, or ventilation."

"Also," added Callahan, "it answers why we weren't taken back like rabbits to be butchered at that testing center."

Harwood nodded, and pointed to a Drumgradian who, with pale and lusterless scales, lay by the gallery wall as if dead. Not yet, however, did either man realize the full severity of the epidemic.

Harwood, meanwhile, was acting as guide through a maze of tunnels. Whenever they saw a gallery that turned upward, he chose it unhesitatingly. "You see," he remarked, "it's like being lost in the woods. If you follow a stream downhill, you're sure to come out somewhere. Same way, if we keep going upward now, we're sure to come out into the daylight."

The winding corridors seemed interminable. Evidently they underlay the entire city in a mighty network, with the aim, the men surmised, of relieving surface congestion.

"Sure, and it's what we'll come to on Earth one of these days," Callahan was ruminating, when a blinking signal just ahead of them caught their attention. Flashing at intervals of about a second, a red light was followed time after time by a blue flare, bright enough to hurt their eyes, yet drawing them on as by a magnet. As they approached, they passed four Drumgradians who lay on the floor, sneezing, wheezing, and coughing.

Just beyond the blinking signal, they were startled by a more brilliant, yellow-white radiance.

"Thanks be to all the saints! The sunlight! I thought I'd never see it again!" rejoiced Callahan, clapping his companion on the back in his joy, while his strained red face beamed. "Now if only somebody dished out a big old ham sandwich, and maybe a good swig out of a bottle, I'd say we were getting on!"

Harwood, trying not to remember his own consuming hunger, muttered to himself, and pressed ahead.

As they reached the blinking light, a disagreeable odor as of decaying vegetables struck their nostrils. Instinctively Callahan shrank back. Then, recovering himself, he reflected, "By glory, I wonder how our own cities would smell to folks from another world." Harwood, just ahead of him, was already pushing out into the open.

Both men blinked, and had to shield their eyes from the light. Staring about them eagerly, they saw a great array of carrot-shaped towers and bubble-like domes looming against the horizon in shimmery faint blue, golden, violet, pink, and milky white. But the nearer scene was less inviting. Bare rocky hills stretched to their left, covered with gray tentlike hovels that flapped in the breeze. On the steep slopes, leveled as by a gigantic plane above piles of boulders and rubble, there were scores of round dark holes into which lusterless lizard shapes flitted as in terror.

"Lord!" gasped Callahan. "Where are we?"

"Just our luck to come up in the slums," groaned Harwood. "Didn't that fellow Orneppu have a name for it? Oh, yes, the Marg! No, the Narg!"

From just to their left, there came a piercing scream, followed by a series of screams as several half-grown lizard forms streaked off into a hole in the ground.

"By gum," laughed Callahan, "we sure must look terrible, to scare the kids like that!"

Hardly had he spoken when, out of other holes at the base of the nearest hill, three oversized lizards darted. Their bodies were of an ashen gray crossed by black stripes. Their flat heads were capped with silvery badges, which, of about half the size of a man's palm, glittered in the sunlight. Their clawed hands wielded triple-branched curved six-foot metallic rods with spear-like points. With snarls and hisses they lunged forward, their tail-eyes shooting out sparks; in an instant, they had surrounded the two men.

"Lord help us now!" groaned Callahan, while the lizards stood glowering about them. "Looks like we're under arrest!"

Harwood scowled, but said nothing.

"I'll say, that's sure a hot one, me being arrested—after all the thugs I've locked up in my time—" Callahan went on, when one of the striped lizards cut him short.

Imperiously, like an officer snapping out an order,

the creature made a sweeping flourish of the spear-pointed weapon, and rasped out several syllables which the men understood clearly enough.

With one of the lizards in front of them, one behind, and the third swinging his triple rod beside them threateningly, they started along a twisting aisle among the tentlike structures. Everywhere, as they approached, shadowy forms scuttled off with screeches of terror. The odors seemed to grow worse. They stared through the tent-doors into interiors entirely bare of furniture. Up and up the hill they wound, puffing and straining; at times Callahan had to pause for breath, while the attendants hissed their disapproval.

Finally they entered a broad roofless enclosure as large as two football fields in one. Its chief features were the rock-walls which, without a break, ascended precipitously on all sides a hundred feet or more, ending in craggy protuberances like the tops of saw-toothed mountains. At the base of the cliffs deep curving hollows, open in front, had been scooped out as if for refuge from the weather. In one corner about a dozen rectangular enclosures, of an opaque gray-green plastic and of about the size of telephone booths, stood blank and conspicuous. On the bare pebbly floor hundreds of lizard shapes were reclining or sat with tails folded under them—miserable-looking creatures, all of them gray and colorless, some with dented scales, a few with closed front or rear eyes, some lacking the usual seven claws on each hand, others with tentacles maimed or chopped off, or twisted or broken tails.

All these creatures, at sight of the strangers, uttered shrill cries of fright, staggered to their feet, and began crowding toward the wall in a panic. But at a few words from one of the striped attendants, they started slowly back to their former positions.

Meanwhile, the foremost attendant jerked a clawed hand toward a bare spot on the floor, just under one of the walls, and let out a snarling sibilant. The hearers did not need to be told that he was commanding, "Down! Down!"

Groaning, they obeyed. As they sank to a sitting position, they noticed that all the nearer natives were shrinking from them.

"Well, George," reflected Callahan, as his heavy form settled down beside the detective, "I can't see that we've been helping ourselves very much. We've simply changed jails."

"Here, at any rate, we do have the open sky above us," Harwood noted, pointing to the sun that glared down almost too hotly from the cloudless blue.

But he could see that they were as hopelessly trapped as ever. To climb the rock-walls was out of the question; and their prison had but one gate, which was blocked by black-striped gray guards. In one corner two jailors, with silvery badges on their heads and long several-pointed blades dangling at their sides, were passing the time by playing a game with green and red counters on a crimson-marked space on the floor.

"Well, anyway," Harwood meditated, glumly, "most likely we won't be here long. They're simply holding us till they can notify the central authorities, after which we'll go back to our former quarters, or maybe somewhere worse, and be made into guinea-pigs again in that damnable testing center."

"Oh, come, old boy, let's not face the worst till we

have to. Just now, George, I'd forgive them devils blue murder if they'd bring me a good fat beefsteak and a can of beer. I'm so hungry I could eat shoe leather."

Two or three hours dragged by while the men's hunger raged more fiercely than ever. Then they heard a great stirring among the other prisoners, and saw a striped lizard entering behind a three-wheeled cart, from which he began to distribute the familiar little brown loaf-shaped objects and the coppery vessels filled with a clear liquid. Everyone shot out his paws for a share. Callahan and Harwood, feeling like animals in a cage at feeding time, joined the others in a pushing impatience; but they were the last to receive their portions, which they consumed so ravenously that the attendants looked on with squeals of wonder. "Sure, even this darned straw tastes like honey now!" remarked Callahan, as he stuffed down the food.

When the meal was over, Harwood's eyes were drawn back to the guards playing their game on the crimson-marked space on the floor. For want of anything better to do, he moved close; and since no one deterred him, he began to watch.

CHAPTER VII

The five young Drumgradians screeched and screamed; excitedly their tails waved and flapped in the big, bare, six-sided, lavender-tinted room. Their half-grown tentacles twisted and wriggled; their scales changed from crimson and indigo to gold-green and violet and then to invisibility; their eyes glittered in many hues. They had surrounded a quarry who, with long red hair flowing loose and deep-blue eyes blazing in rage and terror, stood in their midst like an animal at bay, trying without much success to ward off their attentions.

One of her tormentors, with the jab of a seven-clawed hand and a shout of delight, pulled at her hair. Another clutched at her sleeve, and yelled joyously as a piece of her dress was ripped off.

Then, when she slapped her abusers in self-defense or cried out in exasperation, a grating laughter rose from five small throats. But when one of the urchins poked a claw between her teeth and she instinctively clamped her jaws down upon it, a howl of pain came from the young persecutor, and, for the first time, he and his playmates shrank back to a respectable distance. But this was of little help to the abused girl. A dull-eyed yellow-scaled adult Drumgradian, who chanced to be looking on, withdrew for a moment, and returned with a corrugated, leather-like strip of dark plastic, and clamped this over Eileen's mouth, holding it in place with wires that ran about the back of her head.

"Heavens!" she groaned. "I'm muzzled!"

The encumbrance, fortunately, hardly interfered with her breathing, but she could not talk except in a thick mumbling.

She glanced again at the screeching, squealing crowd, and recalled how, for a period that seemed many days long—ever since being separated from Ted and the other men—she had been here as a plaything of the lizard children. In some ways, she had not been badly treated—she had been given food and drink enough, though it was tossed to her like old bones to a dog; and she had had a dry, warm corner of her own on some straw-like substance in the great hall where all the children slept. There she had had the company of a fellow pet answering to the name of Bung-Bung—one of the six-legged, crocodile-like creatures she had seen roving on the city streets. This animal, about seven feet long, was tame and docile to the children, but snarled and snapped whenever Eileen came near; she could see a suspicious, even a jealous light in its four eyes, and was constantly in fear that its lashing tail would bowl her over.

One of the worst features of her captivity was that she could never get used to the length of the days and nights. The Drumgradian day, she had found, lasted about thirty-six Earth-hours; hence she would often fall asleep when she was expected to be awake, but could not sleep through much of the endless eighteen-hour nights, though she gave thanks for these periods of relief from her young torturers.

"God, how long will it last? How long? How long?" she moaned, as she heaved and panted in the vain effort to throw off the muzzle. Half without realizing it, she murmured one word over and over again, "Ted! Ted! Oh, Ted, when will you come? When will you get me out of this?"

She would not have been much consoled could she have seen Ted at that moment. He sat alone in his little purple-lighted room, straining his eyes over one of the silvery writing tablets. In a way, he told himself, the Drumgradian language was very simple; it had no grammar, no conjugations or declensions such as had always made foreign languages a horror to him. Everything was plain and matter-of-fact; already he and Orneppu could exchange a few words in Drumgradian. He would do his best, in the hope of soon getting out of this loathsome jail.

Wearying of his practice writing, he turned to the television-like screen, where moving objects could be seen as if in three dimensions. Pictures of scintillant domes and fountain-filled avenues flashed before him in rapid succession. But as he stared at those streets, on which occasional lizard forms were moving, he was surprised at the change that had come over the natives. Instead of flitting about with bird-like swiftness, they walked slowly, uncertainly. Some of them paused, racked with spasms of coughing; now and then one fell to the pavement, and rose only when helped by a companion.

At first, however, Ted did not realize how serious matters had become—not, in fact, until about thirty-six hours later, when Orneppu did not arrive at the usual time with the daily rations of food and drink. When at last the attendant did come, several hours late, he staggered as if drunken, coughed in a loud, racking way, and apologized, haltingly, "Earthling, Earthling, for this once—you cannot have your instructoring. I am not well."

He coughed again. Ted, aghast, waited for him to go on.

"I—I cannot understand it. It is like a curse. Some great evil tears at me—at many of my people—and makes us hot all over."

He turned aside to sneeze, and a purplish slime fell from his tentacles, which looked contused and swollen. Then, with eyes that lacked their usual luster, he faced Ted again. He spoke hesitantly and reluctantly.

"Worst of it all—worst of it, Earthling—is that our great Trivate, our noble Olero—has been struck down."

"Oh, but surely he will recover."

Orneppu coughed once more.

"Of course! He still has not lived half of our usual two hundred thousand days."

The speaker was finding words difficult. His voice had a heavy, guttural quality.

"As yet—as yet you do not know all, Earthling. This sickening—she has gone to Olero's tentacles."

"Gone to his tentacles?"

"She has gone to the tentacles of many people. They have swelled so much we cannot use them. The Trivate cannot send out messagings. And without messagings, he cannot rule us."

Orneppu paused, and was convulsed by a succession of sneezes. "Most of us—we could not hear the messagings now, even if the Trivate sent them."

Ted was beginning to understand the extent of the misfortune. The finely balanced sending and receiving organs of the Trivate and his sub-officials had been disabled by the cold which the natives had caught from Harwood, and, as a result, the system of communications had been disrupted. Worse still, unless some way were found to check the epidemic, the entire system of life might soon be out of order.

At this thought, a sharp fear shot through Ted. If the natives were to suspect where the disease came from—and could they help suspecting?—well, Ted remembered how we on Earth treated rats that we had found to be the source of a plague.

But a second, more immediate dread clutched at the prisoner. If anything should happen to Orneppu, Ted might remain unattended in his little room, and die there of hunger or thirst.

"Listen to me, Orneppu, and your sickness will not be very serious," he advised, with deep concern in his voice. "Lie down. Rest all you can. Keep very warm. Drink much water. In a day or two, the swelling in your tentacles will go down."

Orneppu groaned and moaned. "I thank you, Earthling. Surely, to act as you say can do no harm."

But a suspicious glint came into his front eyes as his lizard head shot forward and he demanded, "Now how, Earthling—how do you come to know this?"

Thinking it best to ignore this question, Ted hastened to ask, "Tell me, Orneppu, have you any pain?"

Orneppu groaned again. "Oh, yes. Yes, indeed. You don't know how my tentacles hurt!"

"Then," Ted went on, remembering the little box of aspirin tablets, some of which he had given to Harwood when his cold was at its worst, "swallow two or three of these. I'll guarantee you'll feel better."

Orneppu inspected the pills with a doubtful gleam in his front eyes.

"Oh, well," he decided, as he snatched them in flexible long claws and stuffed them down his toothless mouth, "surely they can't make me feel much worse."

A little later, a glow came back into his eyes and his tentacles began waving excitedly. "Ah, now," he rumbled, once more in his old sonorous voice, "now I understand one of your Earthling words that always gave me much puzzling. Magic! This is magic! My pain—she is gone!"

Muttering thanks in Drumgradian, he flashed into invisibility. It was another day—a full thirty-six hours—before Ted saw him again.

"Earthling," his booming voice filled the little room upon his return, "you are what we call a *Nujeema*—a worker of wonders. Not only has the pain in my tentacles not come back, the swelling has gone down. See for yourself! I am nearly well again!"

As Orneppu displayed his tentacles, which looked much less contused and almost back to normal, Ted inquired, "Then you took my advice—about keeping warm, and drinking liquids?"

"Why not, Earthling, after you drived out my pain?"

He hesitated; nervously flapped his tail against the floor; coughed slightly, and went on, "Truly, this might help my brother Drumgradians, if they took your advice."

"Well, won't they?"

Orneppu growled, "No, Earthling, they say I am not a *Zyreppoq*. Translationed into your language, that is a body caretaker—a healer of wounds."

"Oh, a doctor?"

"Well, not quite, since we never have any sickenings except accidents and old age. *Zyreppoqs* fight these, and keep us in the best conditioning. Theirs is an ancient, most honored skill. So when I told how to heal the coughing trouble, everybody laughed. 'Who are you?' they asked. 'When did you become a *Zyreppoq?*' "

"But couldn't they see that you'd gotten better?"

"Yes, truly. But they said that was because of the good genes—the resisting I was born with. So all my friends took the *Zyreppoqs'* advice."

"What advice was that?"

Orneppu grumbled a curse in Drumgradian. His tail, thumping against a wall, flashed scarlet and orange from its blinking eye.

"The *Zyreppoqs* all say that, since the sickening makes everybody too hot, the cure is cold. The sufferers must chill themselves, so as to drive out the heat. No one must drink water or any liquid."

"But they'll get worse!" protested Ted, who knew that the Drumgradians, unlike reptiles on Earth, were warm-blooded.

"True, Earthling! They *are* getting worse. As I came here, I saw hundreds lying in the streets, as weak as babes still in the eggs. However, the *Zyreppoqs* have an explaining. Their advice has not been followed well enough. Now the people turn on the—what do you call them?—"

"Refrigeration machines?"

"Well, machines to make cold air. They make all their houses so cold I shiver when I go in. But the *Zyreppoqs* say they are still too warm."

"Well, no wonder the disease spreads so fast!"

"Just before I came here," Orneppu related, while ranging the little room with tail lashing, "I saw our noble Trivate, Olero. He was lying on the floor. His tentacles were so big you would not even know him. Four *Zyreppoqs* were treating him, blowing cold air over him from an ice-machine—which made me sneeze and cough again. Olero's tentacles could make no more flashings. He could only speak in the old mouth way, and then very slowly. It was hard for me to hear him. But what he said, Earthling—what he said, she is bad news—very bad."

"How bad?" demanded Ted, with a stab of fear.

"Earthling," Orneppu boomed on, in sepulchral tones, "you have been one of my most favorite charges. I always had a good feeling for you, though I much pitied you for being so weak and helpless. Now that you have cured my sickening, I feel much gratefulness—which, according to an old saying—"

"Come, come," Ted broke in, impatiently, "what was the bad news?"

The Drumgradian's eyes flashed red fire. "I was just coming to that. I wanted to say that, in my gratefulness, I would not wish you to suffer, least of all to suffer—I do not know your word for it, but our word is *Thranku*."

"What's that?"

"It is to be—well, pushed out of life."

"Oh! Killed?"

"Well, yes, in your Earthling language. We

Drumgradians do not put things so crudely. *Thranku* is—well, suddenly not to be any more."

His fists shaking, Ted started forward in a tumult.

"You mean, Olero wants to wipe us out?"

"Now if you will listen to me, Earthling, you will find out." Orneppu's tail sparkled with green and violet lights and threshed about meaningfully before he slowly resumed, "When the sickening started, our people wondered where it came from. Some of us remembered that some of your friends had the same symptoms—"

Ted groaned, recalling Harwood's cold.

"So we knew, Earthling, where the sickening came from. Some said you did not mean to bring it. Others held that you carried it to affliction us. I myself, I do not hold this belief, but I could not make anyone agree with me. The Trivate says that, whether you meant to give us the sickening or not, you are a menace. So as soon as he gets well enough to send out the messaging, he will order *Thranku* for all Earthlings."

"Good God!" groaned Ted, thinking of Eileen more than of himself. "How under heaven will we get away?"

"I know nothing about your brother Earthlings!" snapped Orneppu, whose color, changing from pale red to gray and then to a deep vermilion, indicated the range of his emotions. "But for you—while there is time, maybe I can help."

"But how?"

"I have not a good plan, Earthling, but I will tell you the best I can think of. Maybe you remember that we passed through an ugly part of our city called the Narg?"

"I remember," answered Ted, who had noted the contrast between this wretched section and the splendor of the rest of the city. "What of it?"

"Well, the Narg, she is the only place where they will not look for you. The Narg, also, is the only section where the people have not taken the sickening. We do not know why—maybe because they live in such bad conditions, and have learned to stand everything. Hiding there, you might be safe."

"But how could I hide there?"

"Well, I have an old friend, whose name is Glyp. Once we were like brothers. He worked for Olero, doing secret work, before he displeased the Trivate by polishing his own scales, as we say—which means, getting things he wasn't supposed to for himself. For this he was sentenced to live in the Narg. If you go to him, and say I sent you, he will help you like one of his own."

But what of Eileen? Ted wondered. What of Harwood and Callahan? In any case, how would it benefit them if he refused aid?

"It is a sad place to live, the Narg," Orneppu droned on. "I myself would as soon face *Thranku.* Still, if you wish, I will show you the way. Come! There is no time to lose."

"Show me the way!" Ted acceded. And as Orneppu pushed a concealed wall panel, an invisible U-shaped door swung open, and Ted followed the Drumgradian out into the purplish reaches of a long curving corridor.

"Earthling, take these! You may need them!" Orneppu went on, and displayed half a dozen small round pink pebbles, each stamped with the image of a three-tailed lizard. "They are called *guppu.* Guard them carefully. Each is worth as much as ten days' labor."

"Oh! *Guppu* is money!"

"Not at all, Earthling!" The Drumgradian, as he led the way through the purple-lined gallery, let out a series of green tail-flashes. "We do not work for these, since every Drumgradian is cared for by his city of province. We win them in a little game managered by our city, Arvandu. The most lucky player wins. I myself—I have been very lucky."

Ted thanked his guide, and for a long while they wound on in silence. From time to time they passed a coughing native who lay flat on his back. As they proceeded, Ted noticed that the air was growing close and heavy—which, Orneppu explained, was due to the fact that the *Nunky,* or air officials, were too sick to attend to their duties.

"Even the *Krink,* who make the synthetic food," Orneppu sighed, "are mostly not working now. No one knows what will happen if this keeps up. Some of us prediction that we will starve. They say the supplies are getting low."

Orneppu sighed again, and started up a slope so steep that Ted could hardly scramble after him. For more than a hundred yards they climbed; then burst into the open in a blaze of sunlight at the base of a shimmering pale-blue and cone-shaped tower opposite a tall rock-wall.

Orneppu, with a skill born of experience, swung open a gate in the wall, and pointed to a wilderness of bare slopes dotted with black openings, rock-piles, and tent-like flapping buildings. "The Narg!" he exclaimed, indicating an alley that twisted like a cow-path among the nearest structures.

"Follow that road, Earthling," he directed, pointing. "Take three turns to the right, then three to the left, then down through the first hole, and you will find yourself in Glyp's home—which, like many houses in the Narg, is underground."

"But how—how convince him you really sent me?"

Orneppu thought for a moment. "Well," he finally said, "he used to have a—what do you call it?—a nickname for me, which nobody else knew. Tell him that Zuzum sent you."

"Zuzum. Zuzum," Ted repeated.

"I myself—as I value my tail, I would not be seen going into the Narg," Orneppu went on, with a shudder. "So I must leave you here."

"But what if the Trivate asks you where I am?"

Orneppu's tail wriggled gleefully. "That will be easy. I will tell him you died of the coughing, and your body was so full of evil odors we cast it at once into the *vaccoro*—which is the great trash-pit where we throw all the dead before burning them. Now, my friend, hurry! If you value your life, hurry!"

"Good-bye—and bless you, Orneppu!"

The Drumgradian had already flashed into invisibility. There was a thudding of retreating footsteps—and Ted found himself alone. Biting his lip, he stared across the desolation, tried to forget the disgusting smell that assaulted his nostrils, and with head thrown up, started forward resolutely. As he took the first turn to the right between the slate-hued, tent-like structures, he heard a scuttling of swift forms just before him. At the second turn, there were shrieks and screams as of frightened children; but thenceforth all was bare and deserted. The pavement rocks were hard and sharp, and hurt him through his composite rubber soles. The air was hot and steamy. "Glyp. Glyp," he kept repeating to himself. "I must ask for him. I must tell him Zuzum—Zuzum sent me."

After three turns to the right and three to the left, he paused in uncertainty. In the street before him, he saw not merely one hole, but four or five. All were equally uninviting. All let out such smells that he had to hold his nose. All were blank and black except for the dim tops of staircases leading down into the unknown depths. Which way should he turn? Had he mistaken Orneppu's directions?

Realizing that if he tried the wrong hole he might have no second chance, he was still hesitating when, several minutes later, a rattling behind him prompted him to swing about.

With a gasp, he saw three huge lizard shapes approaching. They were all of an ashen gray crossed by black stripes; their heads shone with silvery badges, half the size of a man's palm; slim curved several-branching, spear-pointed rods, about six feet long, bristled from their clawed hands. With snarls and hisses, they drew near, moving with astonishing celerity; and before Ted could slip away, they had surrounded him.

"Krimgu! Krimgu! Krimgu!" they shouted—and he understood just enough to know that this meant, "You're arrested!"

"What for?" he shouted back. "What have I done?"

The answer was a burst of grating laughter, and he did not know if this was because of what he said, or because of the way he said it. If only he had not hesitated so long! If only he had followed Orneppu's advice to hurry!

The foremost of the Drumgradians, striding within

three paces, was bawling a command. "Come! This way!"

Then suddenly Ted remembered the small stamped pink pebbles given him by Orneppu, and an idea flashed over him. Perhaps the guards resembled some of their species on Earth! Hopefully, therefore, Ted held out several of the pink pebbles.

Immediately the tails of all the Drumgradians began to flash scarlet, and lashed up and down. Their stripes changed to ruddy red, then back to black, then again to red. Their tentacles writhed and twisted. Their front eyes glittered with ruby fire. "Guppu!" they screeched. "Guppu! Guppu! Guppu!"

At the same time, a seven-clawed hand swung out, and seized the pebbles, which all three Drumgradians began to examine by turns with their front eyes and their rear. "Guppu! Guppu!" they continued to cry. "Guppu! Guppu! Guppu!"

Then, wheeling toward Ted and bringing his tail down with a smack, one of them demanded, shrilly, "Where did you get these?"

"They—they—a friend gave them to me," Ted gasped, lapsing into English in his confusion.

"Bling bro blup! Bling bro blup!" came the Drumgradian's sharp reply, which Ted, unhappily, had no trouble in translating. "Thief! Thief! Thief!"

It was useless for him to deny that he had stolen the pebbles. The angry red glitters in fifteen eyes showed that he had been not only accused but judged. He knew that the evidence must seem strongly against him—how, the Drumgradians would ask themselves, could a stranger from another planet obtain these valuable stones unless he stole them?

Now the seven-clawed hands were reaching into his

pockets for the remaining pebbles, which the guards displayed to one another with continued cries, "Guppu! Guppu! Guppu!"

Then, swinging a long curved spear-pointed rod, the head Drumgradian rasped out an order—and Ted found himself dragging his way through the twists of the alley with one guard in front of him, one behind, and one at the side, while the blades of all three swung in his direction with threatening jabs.

CHAPTER VIII

"You know, Chief, that's a darned interesting pastime," remarked Harwood, as he stood watching the game which two guards were playing on the crimson-marked space of the prison floor. The game was played with seven finger-sized and finger-shaped red counters and seven green; each of the players in turn moved the counters of one color around a long oval course marked with various lines, curves, and triangles—obstacles evidently meant to be surmounted. Tense as dogs guarding their bones, the players stood over their counters, and every time one was moved, they uttered low grunts, squeaks, and quick excited cries.

"Don't you see, Chief," Harwood expounded, "the red and green are racing each other, trying to see who can get around that course the fastest. Naturally, there are rules they have to follow, but I'm beginning to get on to them. Why, with a little more watching, I think I could play that game myself."

"Like fun!" scoffed Callahan, spitting in disgust. "As for me, old man—I know I've sunk pretty low, but you can whack me good and hard if I ever want to play with a lot of low-down lizards!"

"But don't you see, Chief, it's a little like chess—and while I don't want to boast, I've won one or two awards at that game," muttered the detective, as he went on watching the contest. Each of the players, he saw, was maneuvering his counters so as to block his opponent, and this took concentration and skill; the competitor had to decide such matters as whether he might be halted by a series of black dots ahead, or whether he could go faster by moving around a rectangular projection marked on the floor, or through the bottleneck of two straight lines.

Hours went by. Four or five games had been played, and the opponents seemed to grow constantly more enthusiastic. They had, of course, observed Harwood leaning over them; but aside from a few contemptuous sniffs, they had ignored him.

At the end of the fifth or sixth game, Harwood stepped forward, rapped on his chest, and repeated the words which he had heard the Drumgradians uttering whenever they had begun a game, "Iko! Ikum! Iko! Ikum!"—which, he surmised, meant, "I too want to play!"

The guards stared at him, and rocked in spasms of grating laughter. Their front and rear eyes blazed with merriment.

"Iko! Ikum! Iko! Ikum!" Harwood repeated, pointing to the crimson-marked space on the floor.

Again a spasm of grating laughter, while the tails of both guards scintillated with yellow flashes.

Reaching down, Harwood took up one of the finger-shaped counters, and moved it forward. "Iko! Ikum! Iko! Ikum!"

Now the guards were laughing slightly less. They began conferring with one another in words that Harwood could not understand, while their eyes flashed green and purple and golden. Finally, still laughing, and with a condescending sweep of a long seven-clawed hand, one of them motioned Harwood toward the red counters. And as he took up the counters and started to play, about half the prison population came swarming around.

"Sure, and how would you feel back home if a chimpanzee wanted to play cards with you?" Callahan afterwards expressed the general feeling. "Maybe you'd say 'yes' just to humor him along and have some fun."

But before Harwood had been playing long, the amused glints disappeared from the onlookers' eyes. He began moving the red counters in an assured way, keeping his pieces not far behind his opponent's. When he committed some breach of the rules—which, in the beginning, would happen frequently—someone would nudge him and move his counters back to the proper position. But he was quick to understand the regulations, and after a time his errors were few. True, he could not match his adversary's skill, and within half an hour he was beaten. His playing, however, had been surprisingly good—so much so that all the guards and many of the prisoners gathered about him with admiring cries, while some expressed their approval by rapping him resoundingly on the shoulder—praise which he felt he could have done without, since the horny hands cut like knives.

"Nu ghee! Nu ghee!" shouted the guards—which meant, "We will teach you! We will teach you!"

Thus began Harwood's favored status. Scraps of a

sweet-scented powdery food, not permitted to most of the prisoners, were given to him, and were duly shared with Callahan. He was also treated to sips of a syrupy liquid, *hazz,* which charged him with an exhilarating new energy. Best of all, he was provided with a device to teach him the language, so that he would be better able to play *Oricha,* the game of the green and red counters. This device, as he described it, was "a picture book and a phonograph all in one"—a plastic roll which flashed pictures of the Drumgradians, their houses, their streets, the parts of their bodies, and other objects. Connected with the plastic roll there was a box of about the size of a large book, in which Harwood heard a whirring as of a disk revolving, while it called out the name of everything upon the roll: for example, "okku" for "leg" or "chinpar" for "scales," repeating the sound slowly several times, and so enabling Harwood to learn rapidly.

Meanwhile, he was mastering the rules of *Oricha,* and had reached the point of beating his opponent in one try out of every three or four. This the Drumgradians held to be phenomenal. They never tired of slapping Harwood on his shoulders (which were now crisscrossed with cuts and abrasions), and squealing, "Holuka! Koluka!" (Wonderful! Marvelous!").

"By glory, old man!" Callahan said, his broad face widening with the old genial ruddy glow, "you're like the prize dog in an exhibition. I'm expecting any day now they'll be tying a red ribbon round your neck!"

But Callahan's lot too had been improved, for he continued to share in the favors doled out to Harwood.

Nevertheless, both men were growing more and more impatient. What, they wondered, had happened to Ted and Eileen? Should they ever see these two again? How could they get out of this monstrous prison, whose monotony was relieved only by the game of *Oricha,* which Harwood played every day, while Callahan could find no respite at all. Then how fearful were the eighteen-hour nights, when they lay in the deep curved hollows at the base of the cliffs, stretched out on the floor, covering themselves with wads of a dirty soot-colored composite, and praying for the daylight!

Even the ordinary nights were bad enough, especially since they were usually chilled to the bone before the first glint of dawn. But when there was a storm, and lightning lashed from the skies, and thunder crashed more fearfully than ever on Earth, and the rain droned down in sheets that splashed even into their shelters—then they clenched their fists, and cursed, and spent hours debating plans of escape, though they well knew that escape was impossible.

Meanwhile, thanks to *Oricha,* Harwood was becoming almost chummy with the guards. After a time, mastering some simple words and phrases of Drumgradian, he was able to ask some of the questions that had been troubling him and Callahan.

"How long are we in here for? When will they let us out?" he wanted to know. And Kryku, an especially big, wide-striped guard, snorted an answer, while nervously curling and uncurling the tip of his tail.

"Who knows how long you are here for? Maybe a hundred days. Maybe a thousand. Maybe they will forget you forever. Why, Bluko over there"—the speaker pointed to a lean old lizard who, with dented gray-brown scales, lay moping in a dark corner of the enclosure—"he has been here more than five thousand days. Nobody knows why he was sent here, not even he himself, but the Black Ones have given no order to free him."

"Who are the Black Ones?"

Kryku rattled his tail in an irritated way. Fierce yellow flashes came into his front eyes.

"That is the name we use for those slimy ones, the Trivate and all his crawling crowd."

These words were spoken in a whisper, which Harwood could hardly follow, while Kryku stared furtively in all directions to make sure he would not be overheard.

"Those slimy tyrants—they keep us under their tails!" the guard went on, warming to his theme. "We have to creep beneath them. They take all the good things." There followed some hearty Drumgradian swearing; then, while his tentacles wriggled excitedly and gave off crimson flashes, Kryku pointed to the craggy precipice walls rising high above them.

"Look at me!" he went on. "Do you think I want to pass all my two hundred thousand days in this hole? But what choice have I? No more than any of these prisoners! The Trivate assigned me to my work because, by some curse of the gods of the three moons Muli, Morbo, and Musken, I was born with the right kind of stripes for a guard. If I objected, I would suddenly be *Thranku*—knocked out of existence!"

"But is there no way to escape?"

The guard's tail came down with a heavy flapping against the stone floor. "Escape? Where to? The Black Ones—they keep constant watch. They see everything, and know everything. They would find us anywhere. Do you not think, my friend, that my brother guards and I and all the people of the Narg have not long wanted to revolt? But other revolts have been put down—and the rebels have all been *Thranku.*"

He paused, took Harwood confidentially about the shoulders with one of his long, seven-clawed hands, then concluded, dolefully, "Not that we might not as well be made *Thranku,* my friend. The Black Ones have all the power, and all the *Guppu,* which gets them whole palaces full of good things. We—we're left the dirt under the palaces!"

With an enraged rasping, Kryku went off to receive a new prisoner who had just been driven in between three long-speared policemen, while Harwood wandered away to watch a game of *Oricha* being played by two guards. But his brow was creased with thought; his eyes hardly followed the movements of the red and green counters on the crimson-marked space.

Not many days more had passed before an unexpected event shook the lives of the two Earth-men.

They had often noticed the gray-green plastic rectangular enclosures, about as large as telephone booths, which stood in one corner of the prison. Sometimes, they observed, one or more of these boxes were removed, and sometimes new ones were carried in, but their number averaged about ten or twelve. What was startling, however, were the noises—the thumps and thuddings, the sounds like wails and moans, which now and then issued from the enclosures.

"Sure sounds like some funny animals are in there," decided Callahan, who, upon approaching the enclosures, had been backed away by a guard.

"Maybe they're animals—and maybe not," replied Harwood, doubtfully. But as soon as he knew enough of the language, he put a question to Kryku.

"Oh, those brutes in there?" answered the guard, flicking his tail contemptuously toward the nearest enclosure. "Keep away from them, or the foul air may poison your lungs."

"Foul air?"

"Those boxes hold only the worst criminals—the *Oodunks,* who are much too dangerous to be let loose. Their evil odors will infect anyone who comes too close. We lock them up all by themselves, until the Black Ones decide what to do with them. Most of them will soon become *Thranku.* Keep away, my friend, I warn you!"

But this explanation only whetted Harwood's curiosity. He continued to eye the rectangular enclosures questioningly—and one day his curiosity was rewarded. A new gray-green plastic container had been wheeled in by two guards, who jested about it with a grating laughter, then left it beside the wall a little apart from the other boxes. From within, some of the usual sounds were proceeding—but with a difference, Harwood noted. He stole as close as he dared, and stood listening. For a minute all was silent; then there came a noise as of someone or something banging and bumping about inside. The noise ceased for a moment, and was resumed, mixed with another sound that sent Harwood reeling back wide-eyed and gaping.

"Damn it! Damn it all! Damn—"

Forgetting the guards, Harwood darted forward. "Ted!" he yelled.

"For Lord's sake, George, get me out!" cried the imprisoned man, after returning the detective's greeting. "There's no air except through some small holes near the top. I'm being roasted alive!"

"How in blazes did you ever get here?"

"They accused me of a crime I didn't commit, and condemned me without a trial. Those dirty lizards—I'd like to murder the whole crazy crowd. Can't you get me out, George?"

"Try my best!" promised Harwood, closely inspecting the plastic surface of the enclosure, which was as featureless as window glass except for a small knob on the upper right-hand side. He was just reaching for the knob when three guards rushed up and waved him off.

"Forbidden! Forbidden!" they shrilled, while several pairs of seven-clawed hands firmly drew him away.

"I myself—I wouldn't care," the guard Quenaquak whispered into Harwood's ears. "But the Black Ones—they have given orders."

As Harwood retreated, he heard a deep groan from the enclosure, followed by a series of heavy raps.

"There's not a thing under heaven we can do before dark—and that's several hours yet," he reported a few minutes later to Callahan. "Then, if I can, I'll try something, though God only knows if it will work."

He slumped down to the rock floor, and, with chin cupped in elbow, sat in silent thought, scarcely seeming to hear Callahan's remarks about how good it would be to have Ted back with them once more.

Not until the long-drawn twilight had given way to night did the detective make any move. Then, when wheezes and grunts and stertorous breathing from all sides showed that the camp was asleep, Harwood tapped Callahan gently on the shoulder, and warily arose. The darkness was not quite complete, for two small pale-gold moons added a faint illumination; the light of unfamiliar constellations shone just above in the gap between jagged opposing cliff-edges; and there was a luminous haze in a wide band where Drumgrade's Saturn-like belt etxended. It was just possible for the two men to go stooping forward very slowly, while Harwood, in the lead, froze into immobility at the faintest suspicious sound or stirring. Once a guard shot up before them with flashing tail-eye; trying hard not to breathe, they sensed rather than saw the slightly crouching lizard form. But he passed on, and still they crept along, and at last drew near the tall shadowy rectangular receptacles.

"Sure you know the right one, old man?" Callahan whispered anxiously.

"Positive! I fixed its position mighty carefully in my mind."

"But suppose they moved it?"

"In that case—well, we'll all be in darned hard luck."

But the rectangular box had not been moved. When the detective had located it and gently rapped, the immediate eager response told him what he most wanted to know.

"George! Thank God!"

"Keep your voice down, you idiot!"

"How are you getting on, Ted old boy?" Callahan could not keep from asking, in syllables that no one could have made out more than a few feet away.

"The Chief, too! Praised be—"

"Quiet, you imbeciles! You both want to give us away?" Harwood unsentimentally broke in.

Suspiciously he stared in all directions, afraid that their speech had attracted attention. But the wheezes and grunts and stertorous breathing still came from all about them and, by drowning their words, may have been their salvation.

"Just a little more patience. There's something here I want to try," Harwood whispered to the imprisoned man as he fumbled for the small knob which he had noticed on the upper right-hand side of the enclosure. In less than a minute, he had located it, and gave it a twist counter-clockwise. But it refused to move. Then he turned it clockwise, but equally without results. He swore softly beneath his breath, and applied added pressure—again to no avail. "Curse the luck!" he muttered to himself. And then, as a final expedient, he pressed down on the knob.

Instantly, from inside the enclosure, there came a faint clattering. Like a window shade when the cord has been pulled, a partition rolled up. The watchers outside could not see the six-foot space which it left clear, but to the man inside it was luminously plain. A second later he had staggered out, and collapsed into the arms of his comrades.

"Don't try to speak yet!" Harwood warned. And after rolling the partition back into place, he and Callahan stretched out the panting form. Harwood felt Ted's forehead, then reached for his wrist, which he held for several seconds. "A few minutes, and you'll be all right," he diagnosed.

"Maybe what you need, old pal," suggested Callahan, "is something to eat. Here, we've brought something—"

Ted made a deterring gesture with one hand. As he afterwards explained, food had been the last of his problems—in his hot, airless hole, he could hardly eat even the little he had been given. "Still, if you hadn't come tonight," he said gratefully to Harwood, "most likely you'd be speaking about the late Ted Hilary. I was pretty nearly suffocated."

Harwood's keen eyes meanwhile, searching the darkness, had spied out a spot near the wall, where they would be some distance from any of the sleeping prisoners. Then, in a few words, he explained to Ted where they were and how they had come to be here. "This is only the opening shot," he went on. "Now that we've got you out of your living coffin, our problem will be to keep you out. I've got a little pull with the guards, but I doubt if I have that much—"

"Then—they might lock me up again?" gasped Ted, as the three of them crouched together in the inky shadows.

"We've got to persuade them not to. First, of course, we'll have to explain how you got out of solitary—"

"And if they think you two did it, you'll be in the doghouse," Ted took up. "Naturally, I can't consent to that. I'll say I managed to release myself."

"They'll never believe it!" snapped Harwood.

"Sure they'll believe it," Callahan demurred. "They'll think he's a magician—a sort of Houdini. Heck, he's better off not to explain nothing. Let them imagine he's got magic powers. Then they'll be too doggone scared to put him back in that box."

"Doesn't sound very practical to me—not unless they're a lot of superstitious numbskulls," grumbled Harwood.

"Listen here, both of you. You don't know how I've been wanting to talk with you," Ted changed the subject, having recovered from his ordeal with surprising resiliency. "There's something that's been worrying me plenty."

Briefly Ted told of the epidemic which had swept the population—a disease whose existence, of course, neither of the others had suspected. "Worst of it," he finished, "is that they blame us for it. An order has gone out from the high muckymuck. All we Earth people are to be *Thranku.*"

"Thrank what?" gasped Callahan.

A shooting star streaked across the heavens. A cloud half obscured one of the pale-golden moons, casting a deeper gloom across the scene.

"*Thranku*—wiped out of existence," Ted explained. "That is, if we don't find some way to escape—"

"God knows we can't escape!" burst out Callahan, pointing despairingly at the jagged precipice top, whose black outlines were barely visible against the stars. "No more than a fish can get out of the ocean! Why, them there peaks—"

"Quiet, you blockhead!" warned Harwood. "Are you in a hurry to get caught?"

Callahan, crushed, became silent.

"There's a good probability," Harwood reflected, keeping his voice so far down that the others had to strain to hear him, "that the high chief's orders haven't yet been received here in the Narg. Our job now will be to make sure that, when they are received, they are not obeyed."

"But even if we can save ourselves," asked Ted, with a despairing note, "how about *her?* How can we save *her?*"

Neither of the others had any answer.

"Why, I haven't the ghostliest idea where Eileen is," Ted went on, mournfully. That is—if she hasn't already—"

He paused; hesitated.

"I know just how you feel, old pal," sympathized Callahan, running a fatherly arm about the younger man's shoulders. "But I've seen some tough things solved in my time, believe me, and I've got a strong hunch this will come out all right."

"Sure, faith is a wonderful thing!" scoffed Harwood. "As for me—I've always found that careful planning gets a lot further."

Without another word, he led the way slowly among the wheezing, grunting dark bodies of slumbering prisoners back to their assigned positions, where they made room for Ted between them in the darkness. They knew that the night still had fifteen or sixteen hours, but to Harwood this seemed not one minute too long for unraveling the tangled problems before him.

CHAPTER IX

When at last a gray cloudy dawn broke over the Narg, the hundreds of prisoners were roused by a blast that pierced their eardrums like a drill. Muttering and moaning, they rose from where they had lain under the plastic floor coverings, folded up these wrappings, and piled them carelessly near one wall. In the twilight dimness, when most of them were still half asleep, they did not notice the slight stirring beneath one of the covers near the farthest section of the wall.

Nor did any Drumgradian hear the whispered words of a brawny, red-faced man. "Just stay there for a while, old fellow, till we can figure out what to do with you."

"The longer we put off those guards," came in a crisper, more rapid voice, "the better off we'll be."

"Well, it's all right with me, boys," said the figure beneath the covers. "I'm so plumb worn out from standing in that beastly cell, I could sleep till the crack of doom."

After a few last words of caution, Harwood and Callahan ambled off to get their morning rations, which were just about to be doled out from one of the three-wheeled carts. "I've always found," said the detective, "when you're stumped, sometimes a yard of delay is worth a mile of action. If only Ted knows enough not to stir!"

"Sure he knows enough!" asserted Callahan. "I'd trust him anywhere. He's a smart boy, Ted is."

But a few minutes later, when they were in the midst of the pitch-and-thrust for the brown bread-like loaves, their plans were suddenly overturned.

All at once the shrill blast, usually heard only at sleeping-time and dawn, was renewed. Varied by a thumping as of a pile-driver and a rattling as of thunder, it sounded for a long while, growing constantly louder and shriller. The prisoners, halted abruptly in their thrust for food, all stood stockstill, leaning slightly forward on their long legs, their tentacles waving, their eyes a-glitter. Excited mumblings came from between many lips; there were squeaks and squeals of fear.

Finally, after the shrillest blast of all, a booming voice burst from a horn placed high on a wall.

"Prisoners, hear me! Prisoners, hear me! A terrible thing has happened! A terrible, terrible thing!"

There was a pause, punctuated by gasps and cries.

"A terrible thing!" the voice repeated. "Something that, should it be discovered, would bring down upon us all the vengeance of his noble Eminence the Trivate!"

Apprehensively Callahan and Harwood exchanged glances.

"A desperate criminal, an Oodunk," the voice droned on, "has escaped. This is baffling, because last night he was tightly locked in his cage. Experts agree that escape is impossible. But this morning, when we went to feed him, the cage was empty. Strangest of all, the cage-door was still locked. How could this be? How did the Oodunk get out? Where did he go? If any of you prisoners know and neglect to tell us, then, by the gods of the three moons, the penalty will be worse than a thousand tail lashes!"

The voice ceased, and fresh murmurs of fear vibrated through the audience. Instinctively some of the hearers backed away, though there was nowhere to go.

"The penalty will be worse than a thousand tail lashes!" emphasized the voice. "Worse, far worse than being made *Thranku!* So now, if any of you know anything of the crime, now is the time to inform us!"

Callahan and Harwood eyed one another more apprehensively than ever, and could not keep their eyes from traveling to a section of the plastic covering near the wall.

"If the culprit is not found, the vengeance of the noble Trivate will smite us all—will smite us all!" the voice droned on; while Callahan, mopping his brow, withdrew beside a pale and worried Harwood.

"Well, I take back all I just said about the advantages of delay," the detective whispered to Callahan. "Way things look now, we'll have to act, and fast, before Ted is found—otherwise, I'm afraid the Almighty couldn't save him."

"Well, we sure can't let him down," said Callahan, flexing and unflexing the muscles of his right arm. "But I'm a brother to one of them there lizards if I see what we can do."

"I've got just the ghost of a plan," stated Harwood.

"Heaven knows, it's flimsier than a paper balloon, but it's all we have. Come, let's get to Ted!"

Owing to the excitement of the Drumgradians, who were squirming about with flapping tails and wriggling tentacles, the two men were not noticed as they wove their way to where Ted lay. They were a little relieved to find the plastic covering above him still undisturbed.

"Wake up, old fellow!" whispered Callahan, peering beneath and giving a poke to the slumbering man, who groaned, looked about him in a startled way, sat halfway up, and began to stick his head out from under the covers—but thrust it back again at a gesture from Harwood.

As well as they could, Harwood and Callahan concealed themselves beneath the covering beside the imperilled man.

"You know, boys," Ted began, "I was just having a wonderful dream. We were all back again on Earth—"

"Listen to me, or we'll all be having a nightmare!" Harwood interrupted. Briefly he told what had happened; then unslung the little black box on his left shoulder. "You know what this is, of course!"

"Sure thing!" acknowledged Ted, who had been taken into the secret long before. "A transistorized tape recorder."

"Very best professional machine obtainable, complete with reel of tape and microphone," added Harwood, snapping out the book-sized apparatus. "It's been my right-hand man in my work. I've recently tested it—the batteries were new, and are still in perfect order. Here! I'll show you how to operate it."

"That won't be hard," answered Ted. "My Dad had one, which I've had lots of fun playing around with. But what in tarnation is your idea?"

From all around them, a new disturbance had broken out. Once more they heard the slow droning voice: "If the culprit is not found, if the culprit is not found, the vengeance of the noble Trivate will fall upon us all. And by the gods of the three moons, it will be worse than a thousand tail lashes!"

The commotion of the other prisoners made it hard to hear Harwood's voice as he rushed on, "We have only one chance. If we can't bluff these lizards—take advantage of their superstitions—then we're done for. Now, Ted, listen!"

After Harwood had finished, Ted smiled wryly. "I get the scheme. It's a long shot—a one-in-a-hundred gamble. We're banking on there not being any recording machines on Drumgrade. Well, count on me to do my best."

As he began fingering the buttons of the recorder, the droning voice resumed in deeper, more hollow tones. "If this criminal is not caught—if this criminal is not caught—"

Harwood and Callahan had begun to make their way back among the prisoners, while the detective looked eagerly for Kryku. It was not long before he saw the big, wide-striped creature driving a crowd of prisoners back from near Ted's former cage.

"Get closer, and you be *Thranku!*" he was threatening.

At the sight of Harwood, he flashed red sparks out of his front eyes, and his tail-eye gave out crimson scintillations.

"It was one of your kind, Earthling," he growled, "who got us into all this trouble with the Trivate!"

"Oh, no, not one of my kind," denied Harwood, "though he has my shape. Listen, Kryku! I have come to help you."

"How can that be?" the guard snorted, as he backed the last of the prisoners away. "Maybe, then, you can tell me how that scaleless beast escaped from a locked cage?"

"I can tell you more than that. I have come to you, Kryku, instead of to one of your brothers, because I want you to get the credit."

"Credit? Credit for what? Have you gone *kertunk?*" Kryku demanded, using an untranslatable word designating a condition halfway between drunkenness and insanity.

"No, but what would you say if I told you we had found the escaped prisoner?"

"I would say you were worse than *kertunk.*"

"Then come with us. Be prepared for a surprise."

His front eyes still flashing red sparks and his tail-eye blinking a deep orange, Kryku started slowly forward. "If you think you can make a joke out of this and live—"

"As I love my native world, Kryku, it is no joke!" swore Harwood, coming close to the Drumgradian, and speaking in subdued tones into one of the dime-sized orifices that served him for ears. "But first I must caution you. The escaped prisoner is no ordinary native of our planet Earth. He is one we honor and beware of. He is what you would call a *Nujeema,* a wonder-worker."

Kryku lashed his tail against the rock floor, and grunted incredulously.

"Then tell me this!" argued Harwood. "How could he escape from an escape-proof cell?"

The red flashes still played in Kryku's eyes, but less energetically. "How do I know you didn't help him?"

"How could I help him? I'm a prisoner myself. I have no tools. But he—he is a *Nujeema*. One flick of his finger can make his enemies *Thranku*. But for his friends he can do marvels."

Kryku muttered something between his toothless gums. "Where," he demanded, "is your *Nujeema?*"

Peeping out from under the plastic covers and seeing the two men and Kryku approaching, Ted pressed a button, which started a faint, almost inaudible whirring in the recorder hidden at his side. Experimentally he set the tape to moving for a few seconds. In one hand he held the bean-sized, skin-colored microphone.

"Ah, by the scales of the Trivate! There he is!" came a low rumbling from Kryku's throat as he pressed on ahead of the others, and turned first his front eyes, then his rear eyes, then his tail-eye upon the fugitive, who had partly disclosed his face. Halting just before Ted and keeping his voice down, he challenged, "Earthling, I have orders to arrest you. The penalty for the crime of escaping—"

"I did not escape!"

"If you did not escape, how do you come to be here?"

"If I did escape, how is it that I am still in prison?"

Kryku swung his long arms forward as if to seize Ted, but Harwood shot into his path. "Do not touch him!" He warned. "He is a wonder-worker, a *Nujeema!*"

"I am a wonder-worker, a *Nujeema!*" affirmed Ted, as he pressed the rewind button of the recorder. "Did I not walk out of a locked cage?"

"Somebody let you out!"

"Who could have let me out? Who knew how? Listen! I can give other proof of my wonder-working!"

"I care nothing for your proof, Earthling! I have orders to arrest you!"

Once more Kryku lunged forward. But as his claws came within inches of the intended victim, he stopped as if frozen. Thundering in his ears, at several times its natural volume, he heard a voice, "Earthling, I have orders to arrest you. The penalty for the crime of escaping—"

The voice was followed by Ted's response and Kryku's rejoinder, all in recognizable tones, though louder than life. The guard shrank back as from a lifted dagger. His tentacles waved. His front eyes were like those of a scared dog.

"Truly," asked Harwood, "is he not a wonder-worker?"

"I—I do not believe it. It is all a trick," argued Kryku, his tail threshing like a hurt snake's in his excitement. "He cannot do it again!"

Seconds later, after Ted had again rewound the tape, Harwood's words followed by Kryku's rang out, louder than before. "I—I do not believe it. It is all a trick. He cannot do it again!"

"See!" pointed out Harwood, triumphantly. "He *has* done it again!"

For several seconds Kryku said nothing. But his great lizard mouth gaped wide.

"Hear me, Kryku!" Harwood pressed his advantage. "I warn you—do not endanger yourself! Do not touch him! A *Nujeema* who can catch your voice out of the air, then make it grow and throw it back at you—"

Harwood noted the squirming of Kryku's tentacles, the agitated tattoo that his tail beat against the rock floor. But he knew that the battle was still not won.

"I—I—it is the Trivate's orders—our Trivate Olero's orders—to catch all escaped prisoners!" Kryku snorted, resuming a tone of menace. "I must not disobey. If I do not arrest him, and Olero learns it—Olero, who is as powerful as the gods of the three moons, and learns everything—"

"Olero will not learn this!" Ted hastily broke in, as the formidable seven-clawed arms again moved toward him. "Have you not heard?"

"Heard what?"

"That Olero has lost his power. He lies on his back, and can hardly move. His tentacles are all red and swollen. They give out no more flashes. They send no messages."

For a moment Kryku stared at Ted in incredulous silence. "Oh, no, Earthling," he denied, "that is too much to hope for. Olero can never, never lose his power!"

All of Kryku's five eyes were flashing at once; and the observers read in them anything but dismay or sorrow. "Wait, I—I must consult my brother guards!" he gasped.

The other guards were at the far end of the prison, two of them playing with the red and green counters on the crimson-marked space, while two others were eagerly watching. Reluctantly, on Kryku's urging, they left the game; and followed him to Ted, whom they observed with shrill excited cries and would have seized had their fellow guard not stopped them.

"He is a *Nujeema! A Nujeema!*" Kryku exclaimed.

"What! A *Nujeema?*"

"Truly. He can catch the voice out of your mouth, and then, whenever you ask it, he can throw it back at you. Never, I swear it by all the towers of our good city Arvandu, was there such wonder-working before!"

Ted, of course, had to prove this statement by a demonstration with the recorder, which he gave at once, to the bewilderment of all the guards, who could only stare, and repeat that charmed word, *"Nujeema! Nujeema!"*

But even more startling revelations lay just ahead.

"Hear me, my brothers!" Kryku hastened on. "The *Nujeema* tells a strange story about our Trivate, Olero."

At the mention of Olero, the glitter in the eyes of all the guards dulled. Low growls came into several throats.

"My brothers, it is too good to be true. I do not believe it can be," Kryku continued. "He says that Olero has lost his power. His tentacles make no more flashes."

The eyes of the guards sparkled again. One of them uttered a long hopeful sigh. "Well, brothers, now that I think of it," he reflected, "not for several days have we had any word from the Trivate. No, not even one small complaint. And that, my brothers, as I value my tail, is unusual."

"Most unusual, Dracu!" agreed all the others.

"Stranger yet," Dracu went on, "we have not even

heard from any sub-ministers, or sub-sub-ministers, who amuse themselves by making our lives miserable. Why, I wonder—"

"I'll tell you why," Ted surprised the guards by breaking in. "The weakness has struck everybody, or nearly everybody outside the Narg. People lie flat on their backs, and are hot all over, and cough and sneeze, and their tentacles are all out of order."

The guards' excitement was growing visibly. "But can it be true? By the red stars of the north, can it be true?" Dracu burst out. "Or do you tell false tales, Earthling?"

"I tell true tales. Go to see, and you will know."

Their eyes shining with ever-changing reds, greens, and goldens, the guards conferred among themselves.

At length Kryku turned to Ted. "If this is true, Earthling, what great changes might it not bring for us all! But we have only your word for it."

"Why don't you investigate for yourselves?"

Kryku muttered a curse. "What do you think would happen to us if we were caught away from our duties?"

"Remember poor old Blynx!" put in Dracu. "He was as good a guard as we ever had, but one day, tiring of life in the Narg, he stole out among the homes of the Black Ones. Poor old Blynx! No one ever saw or heard of him again."

The other guards joined Dracu in a long-drawn sigh.

"Now, Earthling, we must put you back in your cage," Kryku decided, reluctantly. "We must not take a chance, the way poor old Blynx did."

As Ted heard these words and saw several clawed hands lifted to seize him, an idea shot into his mind.

"Listen!" he proposed. "If you yourselves cannot investigate, I know someone."

It was a wild notion, but he had remembered Orneppu's friend Glyp, who, Orneppu had claimed, would do anything whatever for Ted on the mention of his old chum's nickname, Zuzum. Having done secret work for the Trivate, Glyp would know all about that official. And having been sentenced by him to the Narg, he would have no kindly feelings toward his former boss. Therefore might Glyp not be just the right investigator?

When he let this name slip out of his mouth, he hardly expected the instant recognition it evoked.

"Glyp? Know him? Of course!" acknowledged Kryku. "Did he not have to report here every day for a thousand days?"

"He is still in the Narg," Dracu added. "That was part of his sentence. I ought to know that, as he must still report to me every twenty days. He lives—let me see—in Quarters 333 Z of the Seventh Under-District. He is very clever, and has had much training in under-tail work—which, of course, is why he was put here in the first place. If you wish it, my brothers, I myself will speak to him."

The other guards grunted agreement.

"Tell him Zuzum sent you!" advised Ted.

"Zuzum. I will tell him Zuzum sent me. So for the present, Earthling, we will not lock you in your cage. But where," Dracu demanded, suspiciously, "did you learn about Olero?"

"Did I not tell you I am a *Nujeema*?"

"A *Nujeema!* A wonder-worker!" echoed Harwood as Dracu, his long striped tail upraised, started briskly away.

CHAPTER X

Two wheezing and coughing Drumgradians, with silvery badges shining on their lizard heads, and tail-eyes blinking like red fireflies, beat with seven-clawed hands at the crescent-shaped door of a large, vermilion-tinted, dome-shaped house. They both had scales of black-striped ashen gray; and both wielded slim several-pointed rods about six feet long, with which they made a heavy clattering on the door panels when, after a minute, no one had answered their summons.

Still no one responded, and the clattering continued and grew louder, accompanied by a shrill whistling from fife-like instruments. Finally, during a pause in this commotion, a groan was heard from inside, and the door turned inward, revealing a dull-eyed Drumgradian with yellowish scales.

Awaiting no invitation, the two striped callers shoved their way in. Suspiciously they glanced about an immense bare eight-sided lavender-tinted room, where several half-grown lizards lay sprawled, one of them coughing uncontrollably. A large six-legged crocodile-like animal ran forward, nuzzling the newcomers' knees, but the mistress of the house shooed it off with an annoyed, "Away, Bung-bung! Away!"

"Where is the Earthling?" began one of the striped intruders.

"Earthling?" answered Xuxto, with a screech of dismay. "You mean the scaleless, tailless one? All day we have been looking, Eminence. We cannot find her anywhere."

The tentacles of the two newcomers waved like streamers in a heavy wind. Their tail-eyes blinked redder than ever.

"You must find her, Xuxto!" one of them insisted, thumping his tail against the pinkish stone floor. "It is the order of our great Trivate, Olero. For the good of our people, all Earthlings must be *Thranku.*"

"But not *our* Earthling! Oh, not our Earthling!" Xuxto protested. "Why, you do not know how she amuses the children. They call her Gi-gi. She is the best plaything they ever had. She keeps them so busy they have no time to fight among themselves. I swear to you, by the blue stars of the south, she is worth three Bung-bungs!"

"That is of no concern to us! What the Trivate says is the law! Come! where is the little beast?" demanded the larger of the black-striped creatures, as he searched the room by turns with his front eyes, his rear eyes, and his tail-eye.

"But I tell you, Eminence, we cannot find her! We have looked all day." Xuxto paused, and her whole form was racked with spasms of coughing. "It is this terrible weakness that has come upon us all. The children—they were so smitten they were not watching, and no doubt our Earthling has slipped away. But she is only a frail thing, with but two eyes and no tail at all. She cannot have gone far."

The intruders hissed their disbelief, and fiercely swung their tails. "We shall see!" snarled one of them, between gasps and coughs. "If you are lying, Xuxto, you too will be *Thranku!* By the faith of the Trivate! we will find where the beast is hiding!"

With Xuxto trailing helplessly behind them, they began a search. Not one cranny of the house did they miss, though it contained seventeen rooms, seventeen courts, and more connecting hallways and galleries than they could count. But as the search continued, a look of puzzlement deepened in their dull little eyes.

"Thanks to some demon, my tentacles are all red and swollen," one of the searchers snarled. "Otherwise, I could sense where that foreign brute is hiding. But no matter! Soon we will come back. As I value my claws, we will come back, and our great Olero's orders will be carried out!"

With a final growl, the searchers went rumbling out of the house, while the wails of the half-grown Drumgradians followed them amid coughs and sneezes. "Oh, but they mustn't take our Gi-gi! Don't let them take our Gi-gi, our Gi-gi! They mustn't take our Gi-gi! Our Gi-gi, our Gi-gi!"

Eileen did not know how many days passed while she watched for her opportunity, but it seemed like weeks, like months. If she could only slip out, she might find her way to Ted, or, at the worst, to Harwood and Callahan, who would spare no effort to protect her. At least, the chance was worth taking. Nothing, certainly, could be worse than to stay here, muzzled most of the time, manhandled and mauled by those half-grown monsters, and threatened by that still more dreadful crocodile beast, Bung-bung. Fortunately, he had no teeth, but she bore several of his claw-scratches on her legs, in addition to the bruises all over her body from the other brutes. Besides, her hair was all dishevelled, and her torn clothes were in rags. She did not, of course, know of the Trivate's order for the extermination of the Earth-people, but even if she had known, she could hardly have been more eager to escape.

Hundreds of times her glance had traveled to the large crescent-shaped door, beyond which lay hope and freedom. More than once, when a visitor jerked it open, she had sprung toward it, but always one of her captors had pulled her abruptly back. Had it not been for the epidemic of colds, her chance might never have come. But now her captors were all so miserable that none of them noticed one day when Bung-bung, who came and went at will, pushed open the bottom panel of the crescent-shaped door and entered without troubling to shut the panel.

Instantly she grasped her opportunity. Being smaller than Bung-bung, she slipped easily through the opening, which she hurriedly closed behind her. With a hasty movement, she threw off her muzzle, which had been carelessly fastened.

Now she was in front of a vermilion-tinted house with egg-shaped windows, on a broad winding street crowned with carrot-slim towers and bubble-like domes, all exquisitely tinted with pale glimmery gold, blue, green, violet, and milky white, and all joined to their neighbors in a unified whole. Involuntarily she gasped, awed by the beauty of her surroundings. Then, keeping close to one of the walls, she started away with shoulders bent low, like a hunted creature, though she had no idea where she was going.

"God help me now!" she prayed, with such a feeling of aloneness that she wanted to cry. But resolutely biting her underlip, she kept on her way, her long unbound red hair hanging loose about her lean tormented face. From time to time, as if for comfort, she uttered one syllable. "Ted! Ted!"

The street was very confusing, for it wound and spiraled in long curves, and was entered by other streets looking so much like it that Eileen could not tell them apart. Had she not been so disturbed, she would have paused to admire their graceful appearance—the buildings shaped like sea-shells, and colored the daintiest pale pink or aquamarine; and the columned temple-like structures that seemed to glow from within with an emerald, ruby, or sapphire light. Here and there many-hued fountains splashed in the bright sunlight, interspersed with great stone statues of tentacled lizards, while flaming red banners waved like fiery signals atop the tallest spires.

Nevertheless, there was something wrong about the city—Eileen sensed this at once. It was not only that she saw very few natives; it was that when she did see some, they were sprawling on the beautiful inlaid pavements, coughing and sneezing, moaning and groaning. She had the impression that somehow the people's normal life had ceased because of the sickness, but she did not realize what the sickness was, since it seemed to be much worse than any colds on earth.

It was, in any case, her good luck that the lizards were too ill to notice her. Once or twice she did come suddenly upon a half-grown native, who threw up his long seven-clawed hands, and ran from her screaming. And now and then she saw one of those terrible six-legged crocodile monsters, which rushed at her with a snort, while she drew back shuddering against a building.

Where was she going? What would happen to her? She had not the faintest idea. As she curved along through the endless streets, she realized how tired she was, and how hungry and thirsty. The day was as hot as in the tropics on Earth, and her head began to ache and she wanted to sink from exhaustion. Occasionally she did pause, resting on the stone stairway of some domed mansion, or crouching on the ground overlooking a pond featured by a floating plant with lacy red-green leaves larger than umbrellas. Oh, how find Ted now? He might hunt and hunt for her, and never know what had happened—never! But might he not be suffering just as she? And even if by a miracle she did live, would she ever learn his fate?

It seemed that hours had passed when, for the fourth or fifth time, she paused to rest. Strangely, it was getting hotter and hotter. She was gasping and panting; she would have given a sack of gold, had she possessed it, for one glass of water. As she let herself drop with a sigh upon the intricately carved step of a big house, she noticed something that made her start up in dismay. Those vermilion-tinted walls—those egg-shaped windows—suddenly it came upon her where she had seen them before! Her ramblings through the long curving streets had taken her in a circle back to her starting point!

At this discovery, her impulse was to leap to her feet and resume her long dreary pilgrimage. But she was so tired that first she must rest—she must rest. Besides, when she analyzed her feelings, she knew that what she felt was not all displeasure. Mingled with her surprise and fear, there was relief—relief at being back in the only place that she knew. She thought of a caged bird she had once had, which had escaped, then came fluttering back to the cage.

It may have been an hour later when a rose-hued, crescent door opened and a half-grown Drumgradian looked out. "Gi-gi! Gi-gi!" he shrieked, his shrill exclamations awakening the girl who lay asleep on the stoop. "Gi-gi! Gi-gi!"

Two or three other partly grown lizards, wheezing and sneezing, came crowding to the door, and joined in the exultant shout, "Gi-gi! Gi-gi! Gi-gi!"

Immediately their seven-clawed hands seized her and dragged her into the house, while she offered little resistance.

At the same time, the young Drumgradians were joined by their mother Xuxto, who had been drawn by the commotion. "Gi-gi! Gi-gi! Gi-gi!" she too cried jubilantly. "Where in the name of the Trivate do you come from?"

Eileen, who had learned only a few words of Drumgradian, uttered just two syllables in reply. "Gup! Huy!" But this was enough. Xuxto, recognizing the words for "eat" and "drink" and marveling that they could be spoken by one of the lower animals, went out and returned with a tumbler of water and some orange-red pills of concentrated food. After swallowing these, Eileen felt much better.

But though everyone seemed overjoyed to see her, what dark mood had gotten into the lizards? Xuxto spoke to the young ones sternly, then motioned solemnly to the girl, and led her out along a winding passageway, down several flights of stairs, and into a hexagonal basement room no larger than an average bedroom. There were no windows, though there were ventilation holes near the ceiling, and a faint light came from the purplish walls. One of the walls was covered by a screen showing a changing scene as if in three dimensions—a wide underground gallery, with great lizards tottering along it.

"Why am I here?" she cried, as a sudden dread suspicion came to her. *"Why?"* True, she had run away, but she did not deserve to be punished by solitary confinement!

Unfortunately, she could not understand the words that Xuxto was pouring out to her. Xuxto, of course, knew that she could not understand; but she was speaking to her just as a human mistress sometimes talks to a dog.

"Now you stay here, Gi-gi. It's the only safe place. Two of the Trivate's detectives were here today. Those horrible creatures wanted to take you away and make you *Thranku.* But down here they will never find you. This den is reached by a trap door they will not discover. It was made in the old days, when there was much plotting against the Trivate. Not even the children know about it. I will not let them know, so that they cannot give you away. Now you stay here, Gi-gi. I will come from time to time, and bring you things to eat and drink."

One of Xuxto's seven-clawed hands brushed the soft flesh of Eileen's arm in the caressing way of a mistress fondling a dog or cat. A moment later, the door jarred to a close, and the girl was alone in the small, unfurnished room.

No longer able to hold back her tears, she threw

herself down on the floor. "What have I done, oh, what have I done to be punished like this?" she wept. This lonely imprisonment was even worse than being with those terrible lizard children. When would she get out? When would she be rejoined to Ted? Her small fists beat against the walls until the blood came . . . before at last, in sheer exhaustion, she fell asleep.

But even sleep gave her no relief. She had a dream of a huge web, whose strands coiled about her like ropes. The more she struggled, the more tightly she was held; while from above her something immense and black, which she could not clearly see, was descending, descending, descending, threatening to clutch and strangle her. . . .

CHAPTER XI

Glyp was a small, slim Drumgradian, with scales that were ordinarily copper-hued but sometimes ranged in color from gray to buff, saffron, and mud-brown. His amber-tinted front eyes glowed with a soft, friendly light, but his steely blue rear eyes had a hard, calculating glitter, while his tail-eye blinked from blue to yellow according to his mood.

It was blinking more vividly than usual as he stood at one end of the prison enclosure, surrounded by five guards. "So it is true? It is true?" they were demanding, as they swung their tails high and brought them down with eager flappings. "It is as the Earthling said?"

"It is as the Earthling said," affirmed Glyp, his long tentacles curling and uncurling. "The gods of the three moons are with us. The Black Ones are stricken by a glorious malady. They lie about, and strange noises explode deep inside them, and they are hot all over, and get weaker and hotter while our healers order icy breezes to blow over them."

The guards exchanged glances. Happy flashes came into their eyes.

"But Olero? Tell us about Olero!" Dracu flung out.

Glyp slapped his tail against the floor, and answered with a snort of satisfaction.

"Naturally, I could not see with my own eyes. I had to keep from being recognized, though, by my scales! few people were well enough to notice me. I went straight to my old friend Orneppu, who, by great good luck, had not the weakness. From him I learned that Olero's tentacles are indeed out of order. He cannot send out messages—"

"The gods be blessed!" interrupted Kryku, giving his big striped form an excited turn, and lifting his clawed feet as if to dance. "Then the Trivate has no longer any power!"

"He no longer has any power! Now, now is the time to strike!" took up Dracu, with a snort. "My claws! we must not wait to pay him back for all we have suffered!"

His eyes flashing a vindictive red, he swung a long spear-pointed rod in one huge hand. The other guards milled about in uncontrollable excitement.

But one of them, Quenaquak, waved his long striped tail high above him in a gesture of caution.

"Take care, my brothers! What if this story be not the truth? By all the meteors of the night! You know as well as I do what Olero's vengeance would be—"

Groans and shudders were his answers. A heavy silence followed.

"Someone else must investigate. At the risk of being caught, I will be that one," volunteered Quenaquak. "It will be worth taking any chance to escape from this wretched Narg, which for ten thousand days I have been unable to leave."

Followed by shrill warnings, Quenaquak started

away. All the rest of the day the guards, no longer playing *Oricha,* stood about in a close knot, whispering and muttering.

Ted meanwhile, returned to his cage and near to fainting from the heat, was too sick to wonder or care much what would happen. He was not even helped by comradely words of reassurance when Callahan, profiting from the preoccupation of the guards, dared to come close. "Cheer up, old fellow, we'll get you out! We'll get you out, believe me! 'Twon't be long now!"

But it seemed long, very long, though probably it was not more than six or seven hours before Ted heard a fresh commotion, and recognized the snorts and rumblings of Kryku, Dracu, and the other guards. Soon afterwards he heard Harwood's voice from just outside his cage.

"Listen, Ted! Quenaquak has just come back!"

"By God," added Callahan's deep, cheerful voice, "they're making such a racket, you'd think they were kids just out of school! That Quen, or whatever you call the devil, sure seems to've brought good news!"

Shouts and roars went up in loud successive waves, a little like volleys of applause at a college football rally.

"Quenaquak! Quenaquak! Quenaquak!" was repeated over and over again by five or six voices, followed by something which, Harwood said, could be freely translated as, "Three cheers for Quenaquak! Three cheers, three cheers for Quenaquak!"

It was only a few minutes later when they heard the guards surging toward them. There came a rattling as Ted's cage door flew open. Feeling more nearly dead than alive, he staggered out amid a confusion of voices. "*Nujeema!* Wonder-worker! The gods of the three moons smile upon us! Quenaquak says you are right! A marvelous weakness has struck down the Black Ones! The great Trivate Olero—he is great no more! He is feebler than a young one with its tentacles not yet grown!"

Again that shout dinned through the air, and echoed and re-echoed like applause at a football rally.

Reeling and trying hard to regain his balance, Ted heard Kryku's voice.

"It is a judgment of the gods! A judgment against the Black Ones—against Olero! It would be defiance of the gods not to use our chance when they have given it! The gods, the gods are on our side! You, *Nujeema,* you must lead us!"

"The gods, the gods are on our side! You, *Nujeema,* you must lead us!" cried the other jailors, as they swung about in circles, their tails waving like those of excited dogs.

"But I—how can I lead you?" gasped Ted, feeling barely able to support himself against the side of the cage. And he had just the strength to utter the word, "Huy! Huy!" meaning, "Drink! Drink!"

A diversion was created while Kryku ran for a tumbler of some refreshing liquid. After Ted had drunk, he felt much better.

Already, fortunately, a dimness was coming into the sky, and some of the brightest stars were appearing in the vague spaces between drifting clouds. This, Ted thankfully reflected, meant a reprieve, for the Drumgradians rarely if ever worked at night. The approaching eighteen hours of darkness, he thought, would not be one minute longer than he needed to rest—to rest, and to think and plan.

In his exhaustion, he soon fell into a deep, refreshing sleep in the place assigned him beside Harwood and Callahan. When he awoke, seemingly long afterwards, the grating, rasping noises of slumbering Drumgradians came to him from all sides. Above him, the rim of an orange-sized moon was just drifting out of sight behind the saw-toothed edge of a cliff. In a clear gulf of the heavens, a bright bluish star was surrounded by a vivid circle of lesser luminaries. Was it in that direction, he wondered wistfully, that Earth rotated, bearing with it the people and scenes he had loved but would never see again?

A heavy voice from his left broke into his ruminations.

"Ah, old fellow, awake at last? D'ye know, more than half the night must be gone!"

"Sure, we thought nothing but the blast of Doomsday would wake you," came the crisp tones of Harwood.

Ted drew himself up rubbed one hand drowsily across his forehead and stretched his limbs, which were still sore and cramped from the long ordeal in the cage. "Well," he yawned, "I wouldn't mind sleeping till the blast of Doomsday."

Callahan had crept close through the darkness, and was speaking almost into Ted's ear. "Didn't like to wake you, old man, but we've got a lot to talk over. Me and George here have been figuring things out."

"It's simply this," Harwood explained, in his rapid-fire delivery, though his voice was hardly above a whisper. "We've got to take our chance when it comes, and it looks to me like it's come now, before those accursed lizards get over their sickness. You heard the infernal commotion the guards made—they're like small boys with their first guns, and we'd better act while their enthusiasm holds."

"Sure, I know that," answered Ted, rolling over on one side so as to face Harwood. "But how can we act?"

"That's where you come in, young man. You're the —what the devil do they call it?—the *Nujeema,* the miracle man. Don't you hear them say you must lead them?"

"Yes—and I'm about as well fitted to lead the fishes in the deep sea."

Callahan choked out a half-formed laugh as a shadowy lizard form listed toward them in the darkness.

"Come to think of it, Ted, we're all in the deep sea," Harwood answered, after the intruder had retreated. "None of us are going to get out without a struggle. If we must take risks—well, the Chief and I think the worst risk of all would be to do nothing. So we've hatched a scheme. Want to hear it?"

Keeping his lips close to Ted's ear, Harwood spoke in a torrent. Until the gray of dawn began to brighten the ragged cliff-edges high overhead, the discussion went on, while gradually a new eagerness came into the voices of the three conspirators. Impatiently they waited until the camp had indulged in the pitch-and-grab for the morning meal. Then Harwood hastened to Kryku, who was just beginning a game of *Oricha* with Quenaquak on the crimson-marked strip of pavement.

"Now's the time!"

Kryku looked up. In his annoyance, his tentacles wriggled like disturbed snakes.

"The *Nujeema* is ready!" Harwood rushed on. "Now's the time! Call a meeting of all the camp!"

"Can't we wait till we finish our game?"

"We have a bigger game to play, Kryku. Olero will not wait!"

His arms swinging in wide gesticulations, Harwood explained his ideas. As he hastened on, the leaden look of Kryku's front eyes gave place to an excited bright yellow; his tail shot up and began swaying back and forth. Quenaquak too was aroused; his tail-eye sparkled; his tentacles gave out crimson flashes. "Call our brothers!" he proposed, and shouted, "Dracu! Krupca! Tyntyl! . . . Dracu! Krupca! Tyntyl!"

A noisy meeting of six guards followed. "As we love the gods of the three moons, we must act!" they exclaimed, in a chorus of screeches and rumblings. "We must act before the Black Ones get the smell of what is happening!"

Hopping over to the nearest wall, Kryku turned a tiny, almost concealed knob. The results were nerve-shattering. There came a blast as if a hundred factory sirens had been joined by pounding piledrivers, roaring and crashing bulldozers, and screeching pneumatic rock-drills. The very ground shook; the precipice walls seemed to waver as if about to fall.

Then, for an instant, the racket ceased. But promptly it was resumed, while the three men, clapping their palms over their ears protectively, observed the results in astonishment.

When the noise began, the hundreds of prisoners had been sitting or lying about as usual—dismal, listless-looking creatures, many of them maimed or with dented scales, many with their tails folded hopelessly under them. But as the loud successive blasts dinned about them, they all leapt to their feet, their tentacles flashing fire, their scales colored with rapidly changing red, orange, yellow, and purple. In thick-packed ranks, they gathered in a semi-circle where Kryku, with a long curved spear upraised, waited to receive them.

Waving the spear to restore order, he waited for quiet to return, then burst into a shout.

"Brother Drumgradians, we have called you for the most important event, the most important in all your two hundred thousand days! You and I are here in the Narg at the orders of the Black Ones. They would keep us here till our scales fall out! Would you not like to be free, brother Drumgradians?"

Even the din of the sirens had seemed to make less of a commotion than the roaring that now broke out. The prisoners shrieked and howled. Their scales turned every color of the rainbow. Their eyes flashed bright green, golden, flame-red. Their tentacles waved and let out sparks. The three men, as they watched, were unable to recognize the drab, woebegone creatures of a few minutes before.

"A great *Nujeema,* a wonder-worker has come among us!" Kryku went on, while the men strained to follow him. "He will lead us! He will lead us to freedom!"

"*Nujeema! Nujeema!* Let us see the *Nujeema!* He will lead us to freedom!" went up a tumultuous cry. And Ted, prodded by Harwood, came forth. But he almost wished to be back again in his cage rather than to face this agitated, tail-waving lizard crowd, which drew so close to him in their excitement that their crushing weight could be restrained only by the thrusting spears of the guards. As he stepped forth, he could feel the foul animal breath hot against his skin.

In the front ranks of the prisoners. a large gray-blue

creature lunged forward until Ted could have touched his battered form. His front scales were nicked and partly broken; the flat rear end of his tail was missing; one of the seven claws on his right side was gone. His forward eyes, as he burst into speech, blazed a menacing red; his tentacles shot out sizzling green sparks.

"Brothers," he demanded of the guards, in tones as piercing as a drill, "let us not be too hasty! What if this is all a ruse to catch us? How do we know the stranger is really a *Nujeema?* What if he is an agent of the Black Ones?"

Defiantly he poked the seven crooked claws of his unmutilated hand into Ted's face, while a growl of challenge and a hiss of contempt escaped from his wide lizard lips.

No one meanwhile noticed how the reels of a small machine in Ted's hand were revolving; no one saw the bean-sized, skin-colored little object at the end of a thin wire. But everybody heard Ted's challenge, "Listen, friends, and you will know if I am a wonder-worker!"

Few if any, amid the commotion, heard the faint whirring of the rewinding reel. But all those in front started back in amazement at the words that, after a minute, came to them from Ted's direction in the voice of the gray-blue prisoner, as loud as before or perhaps a little louder:

"Brothers, let us not be too hasty. What if this is all a ruse . . ."

Word for word the speech was repeated, even to the growl of challenge and the hiss of contempt at the end.

"See!" Kryku triumphantly pointed out. "He can catch words out of the air and throw them back! Is he not truly a *Nujeema?*"

"Truly, truly a *Nujeema!*" several voices echoed.

Only the gray-blue prisoner appeared unconvinced. "By the ring around our planet," he scoffed, "you are being fooled, my brothers. He is no more than a clever mimic!"

He paused, while an excited murmuring filled the air. Then he flung his challenge: "Can he throw *these* sounds back at me?"

Deliberately, amid a harsh grating, he scraped the stone pavement with his claws. Then he thumped his tail—or, rather, the remnant of his tail—three times against the pavement. Finally, he slapped his claws together with a peculiar clattering and rattling.

"Can he throw these sounds back? If so, he is indeed a wonder-worker!"

Half a minute passed in silence, except for the low whirr of the rewinding reel. Then, at their natural speed, the grating of the claws, the thumping of the tail, and the other background noises were all faithfully repeated.

There was silence for the fraction of a second, followed by cries, *"Nujeema! Nujeema! Nujeema!"* while the gray-blue one retreated with tail drooping in defeat. "The *Nujeema* will lead us forth!"

"I will lead you forth!" promised Ted, in his loudest tones, while hoping that his hearers could not know how fiercely his heart was beating.

It was Kryku who, at this crisis, came to the rescue. "Brothers," he shouted, "I call for volunteers! I call for volunteers! Who will join us? Who will follow us into the haunts of the Black Ones? Who will side with us against the Trivate Olero? All who will join us, lift your tails!"

The answering roar was minutes in dying down. When at last it had subsided and the lifted tails had been counted, Kryku made his announcement. "It is as I had hoped! All of you, my brave brothers, have volunteered!" The only exception was one poor creature who lay in a corner with closed eyes and feebly swaying tentacles, too old and weak to lift his tail.

"As I love my scales, brothers, you have proved your courage!" commended Kryku. "Now will you swear, by the tails of your ancestors and the gods of the three moons, you will not desert our cause but will loyally go wherever I and the *Nujeema* lead! Remember, before you swear—the gods of the three moons will take terrible vengeance on any oath-breaker!"

"We swear it! We swear it! By the gods of the three moons, we swear it!" burst forth a tumult, while tails flapped and tentacles swung wildly in air amid red and orange sparks. "We will follow you! We will follow the *Nujeema!*"

"Touch your tentacles to the pavement! Swear it again!" insisted Kryku. "Swear it by all the stars of the night and the gods of the three moons!"

Each struggling to be first, the prisoners stooped, and scraped the stone floor with their tentacles. "We will follow you!" they repeated. "By the gods of the three moons and all the stars of the night, we swear it!"

"If you are not faithful, may you be torn until not even your scales remain!" Kryku finished for them, with an ominous rumbling. "Now we go forth!"

There was a surge forward as two guards turned a series of levers and the great clanking slate-gray metallic prison gates swung open, leaving an avenue through which the lizard shapes could stream ten abreast into the free spaces of the Narg.

At their head strode Kryku and Ted. Harwood and Callahan kept pace beside them, while Glyp marched just to their right, and Quenaquak and several other guards moved on the flanks of the crowd to maintain order. In Ted's right hand was a long, five-pointed, curved spear which Quenaquak had given him.

"Down with the Black Ones! Down with the Black Ones! Down with Olero! Tear his scales off! Chop off his tentacles! Down with Olero! Forward, forward for the rights of plain Drumgradians!" chanted the rabble, with fierce enthusiasm. Their scales still flashed with many colors and their glittering eyes continued to give out vivid red and orange sparks, offering no reminder of all of their recent dull, disheartened condition.

"By gum, old man, looks like we've got a real revolution on our hands," Callahan whispered into Ted's ear as they passed out into a region of gray tent-like hovels perched on desolate hills above piles of boulders and rubble. "Well, if you need any help, you can rely on me—"

He pumped his muscular right arm up and down reassuringly, and his round red face glowed with enthusiasm.

"We're going to need all the help we can get," reflected Harwood, his greyhound face looking cool and unconcerned, though there was a glitter in the deep-set eyes. "A revolution, I'm afraid, is like the proverbial snowball rolling downhill. It's easy enough to start, but heaven knows where it'll end."

"Down with the Black Ones! Down with the Black

Ones! Down with Olero! Tear his scales off! Chop off his tentacles! Down, down with Olero!" the marchers still bawled and bellowed.

And now, from all directions, other cries eagerly answered them. From the flapping tent-like hovels and from holes in the ground, the residents of the Narg swarmed forth at the sound of the scores of passing demonstrators. "Down with Olero!" they joined in shouting. "Down with Olero! Forward, forward for the rights of plain Drumgradians!"

Short or tall, fat as young bears or slender as does, spotted like leopards or mottled like autumn leaves, shifting suddenly from invisibility to visibility, the Nargites were more varied in looks than the men had realized. Many of them, with ever-changing hues, had been transformed startlingly from the gloomy wretches of a few minutes before. Ted noticed with surprise that not a few, with large bright eyes and heads much less flat and wedge-shaped than those of other Drumgradians, were the most attractive he had seen on this planet.

Singly and in groups, until they were numbered by the hundreds or thousands, the Nargites kept crowding out of their dens and shanties, while joining in the cry, "Down with the Black Ones! Down with Olero! Tear his scales off! Forward for the rights of plain Drumgradians!"

"By jiminy, boys, we've got an army!" Callahan summarized, as the multitude still pushed on beneath the desolate hills.

"Unfortunately, an army without weapons," pointed out Ted.

"I don't agree with you," denied Harwood. "Those seven-pointed claws and swinging tails—personally, I wouldn't care to meet them in combat. Besides, notice over there!"

His keen eyes had detected what the others, amid the confusion, had not observed—a corps of large Drumgradians, each armed with a heavy stick or stave. Just beside them, several of their comrades were demolishing one of the tent-like little houses, and tearing its posts out of the soil. Meanwhile, scores were combing the ground for rocks, which they dropped into little pouches at their sides.

"Good Lord, where are we going now?" asked Ted. Though he still marched at the head of the tumultuous column, he gladly took any direction Glyp indicated with a claw-flick.

"We're leaving this filthy Narg, my boys," Callahan jubilantly decided, as the howling, tail-flapping multitude reached a sharp turn at the base of one of the hills and saw the carrot-shaped towers and the great shining bubble domes rising just before them. Separating them from the favored districts was a tall wall composed of seemingly impassable rock—the first of the three barricades that they had noticed from the moving platform which had carried them to see the Trivate. Beside the wall, in front of a closed gate, three striped guards lay wheezing and gasping.

Almost before he realized what had happened, Ted heard a triumphant shout from beyond the wall. Several of his followers had buffeted the guards aside, pulled the unlocked gate open, and entered the forbidden regions. An instant later, the army was swarming in after him.

CHAPTER XII

Like wild beasts escaped from their cages, the Nargites raged through the streets. They surged through the fan-shaped and crescent doors of the daintily colored, iridescent buildings, and emerged with claws full of bright-colored loot. They flung rocks that shattered shimmering plastic windows, their sticks battered down the brilliant scarlet flowers and vivid twelve-foot grasses, they smashed the fountains and the great lizard statues, and mauled and beat all of the inhabitants they could find—which is to say, all who were too sick and weak to escape. "Down with the Black Ones! Down with Olero! Off with his scales! Forward, forward for the rights of plain Drumgradians!" they continued to chant.

Shocked and shaken, Ted raised his arms and yelled at the top of his voice to check the outrages. But no one seemed to hear him. No one seemed to care. He might as well have cried out to halt the gale.

"Let them have their way!" Harwood shouted into his ear. "Every revolution has its price. The poor devils have been kept down so long—it's like a kettle when the lid blows off. Be thankful they're not letting steam off against us."

"Believe me, I wouldn't want to be in that guy Olero's shoes when they get their claws on him," Callahan contributed. "He won't be worth his weight in mincemeat."

"Sure, but they haven't got him yet," cautioned Harwood. "Do you think a wily old dictator like that hasn't foreseen a possible revolt and done something to protect himself?"

Surely enough, it was not long before they had reached the second of the three walls which they had observed from the moving platform. Dark-green and imposing as a fortified medieval town, it stretched to the height of a three-story building as far as they could see in both directions. Covered with hard, sword-shaped leaves that swayed back and forth slowly and menacingly as if controlled by invisible hands, it was unbroken by any gate or window. To make things even worse, the edges of the leaves were toothed like saws and razor-sharp, as one of the marchers learned when he leaned too close and his foremost tentacle was sliced away while he withdrew with a shriek.

"Down with Olero! Down with the Black Ones! On for the rights of plain Drumgradians!" the mob still chanted, while some were already attacking the wall with rocks and clubs. But the more fiercely they assailed it, the more threateningly the armored leaves thrust out at the attackers, disabling half a dozen under apparent intelligent guidance.

"Good Lord!" Ted groaned. "I'm a cousin to a donkey if I see how we're going to break through!"

"We'd better break through," Harwood muttered, grimly. "You don't think, do you, that after what we've started, that fiend of a Trivate is going to smile politely and pardon us?"

At this impasse, when the howling multitude still pushed on as if resolved to beat itself to death against the wall, rescue came from an unexpected source. Waving his screeching fellows aside, Glyp slid a few paces to the right, where the sword-leaves seemed thickest and most menacing. With three hasty thumps, his tail pressed down on an almost invisible plaque in the rock pavement. And instantly a groaning, a rattling, and a rumbling was heard, and a gate appeared in the wall of leaves.

"It was not for nothing," Glyp whispered to Ted, "that I used to work as a secret agent of the Trivate."

More than ever before, Ted now realized why an individual who knew as much as Glyp had been banished to the Narg.

"Down with Olero! Off with his tentacles!" screamed the mob, as it swarmed through the gate. "Down, down with the Black Ones!"

But before the marchers had gone many hundreds of yards farther, an even more imposing obstacle loomed in their way.

Glittering and smooth as glass, the third wall rose more than a hundred feet. Its beetling sides were bottle-green, and unmarked by any foothold for scaling; its top was lined with long, down-turning, daggered spikes. At intervals of about an eighth of a mile, squat towers projected as from a fortress. And, along its base, a moat as wide as a wide city street was filled with stagnant, dark, scum-covered, ill-smelling water.

On the banks the rebels halted. Many dispersed to loot the nearby mansions, from which they returned weighed down with boxes of food and casks of drink, while pandemonium arose as the raiders clawed one another and fought for their shares amid shrill cries and threshing arms and tails.

"Glory be, how're we going to handle this, old man?" Callahan threw out at Ted, who stood leaning on his spear, gazing at the barricade in a stunned way. "No self-respecting cat would try to get up that wall."

"Nor any circus acrobat," added Harwood, glumly. "We'll have to go around it."

"You can't go around!" warned Glyp, who had not understood the words but seemed to guess their meaning. "It encircles the whole district without a break."

Just then one of the Drumgradians, whose enthusiasm exceeded his judgment, created a diversion by splashing into the moat and swimming toward the opposite bank. But after a few yards, he turned with a scream and started back at great speed. As his comrades pulled his sputtering form out of the water, Ted caught sight of a black snake-like triangular head larger than a bull's, which shot out of the water, while a gigantic hump, like a dromedary's back, lifted itself above the surface and disappeared fifty or sixty feet behind.

An awed silence settled over the watchers as a tall wave, from the monster's passing, rolled from side to side of the moat.

"Lordy, lordy, wouldn't it be nice to have that little fellow for a pet!" exclaimed Callahan, after a moment. "Well, believe me, boys, I'm not going swimming today!"

Bleakly the two other men exchanged glances. "Surely, there is some way of getting through the wall," Ted appealed to Glyp. "Some hidden lock you can turn."

Glyp thumped his tail against the rock pavement in vigorous denial.

"Unfortunately," he answered, his front eyes glowing from amber to dull red, while his tail-eye blinked on and off uncertainly, "that is what is known as *nu-chi-nuchi,* or deepest-deepest-deepest secret. The two outer walls—they do not matter so much, which is why I was allowed to know their secrets. But this inner wall—it is the Trivate's most guarded defense."

Forced to a halt, the marchers were milling about restlessly. "Down with Olero! Down with Olero! Off with his tentacles!" they still roared, to keep up their own spirits. Scores of them, ranging farther and farther afield, were still busily plundering the palaces; others wriggled about amid the smoke of great fires, while heaps of drapes and hangings, gaudy chests and chair-like furnishings were being burned for the amusement of the screeching crowds.

Feeling like an inexperienced climber called upon to scale Mt. Everest, Ted reflected on Glyp's dismal words. "You mean to say," he demanded, "we can't get around the wall, we can't get over it, and we can't get through it?"

Glyp's tentacles twisted so rapidly that Ted could hardly follow their movements, while they gave off a sputtering of green and golden sparks. "True," he acknowledged, with a hiss. "But that still leaves one possibility."

"What can that be?"

Swinging his copper-hued form along the edge of the moat with a squirming movement, Glyp turned so that Ted could see the hard, calculating glitter in his steely blue rear eyes.

"Scales of the Trivate! is it not clear?" he squeaked.

"If we cannot go over, around, or through, then naturally we must go under!"

"Under?" threw back Ted, with visions of laborious tunnelling operations. "How can we go *under* the moat and the wall?"

Glyp whirled completely around, flapping his tail almost in Ted's face. "Maybe you do not know," he expounded, "of the underground galleries leading from building to building. Some of these reach from the Trivate's palace even into the Narg. They are narrow and badly lighted, and are known only to a few palace officials. Of course, they are ordinarily guarded. But now, all the guards being too weak to watch them—now, Earthling, there is a chance that we can get through."

"I remember them very well," acknowledged Ted, picturing the winding, purple-lighted corridor that had taken him to the Narg. "But how get an army through those small passageways?"

"Did I say we must get an army through?" snapped Glyp. Slowly and soberly he wandered on. "Now, if ever, is our time! Remember, since leaving the Narg, we have met only a few people, who were too weak to stop us. But there is something still stranger. Usually big black-striped sentries stride on the top of the wall. Do you see any of them now, Earthling?"

He pointed to the spike-lined rim of the wall, and to the nearest of the squat towers. But Ted saw no one moving there.

"The sentries all have the weakness," Glyp concluded. "Surely, the gods of the three moons favor us. Now there will be no one to warn Olero. True, Earthling, it is a deadly risk even now—a deadly risk! Are you willing to take the chance, knowing that, if we are caught—"

"I would take a chance with my very neck!" swore Ted, whose thoughts were not on Olero or any of his henchmen, but on two haunting deep-blue eyes framed by red hair.

"Then, Earthling, hear my plan! And thank the three gods that I know the way to one of the passages under the wall!"

Glyp bent close to Ted, his amber-tinted front eyes gleaming; and for a long time the two and Harwood stood conferring, while the din of the marchers still rang in their ears, "Down with Olero! Down with Olero! Down with the Black Ones! . . ."

Finally, having reached a decision, Ted turned to Kryku, who had been trying to restrain an excited group from ripping some yellow and vermilion streamers from a building opposite the wall. "I must leave for a little while," Ted reported. "Meanwhile, you must take charge here. Now will you pick six of our ablest followers?"

A few minutes later, Ted started off on a curving side-lane away from the wall. He was still wielding his spear; Harwood, Callahan, and Glyp strode beside him swinging clubs. Just behind them rumbled six lizard creatures, all brandishing spears or staves, and all with waving tentacles that shot out sparks, while their eyes by turns blazed a fierce deep red, a fiery orange, and an intense baleful green. "Down with Olero! Down with Olero!" they echoed the cries of the multitude. "Forward for the rights of plain Drumgradians!"

CHAPTER XIII

Back and forth, back and forth, back and forth the imprisoned girl paced on the stone floor of her small, purple-lighted room. Already, it seemed, she had been here for years, for centuries. At intervals she had been visited by her mistress Xuxto, who had been kinder than you would expect of one who had punished her so unjustly. Regularly she had brought her food and drink, and often had stroked her with caressing claws and spoken to her gently, though in words that she could not understand.

But most of the time the prisoner remained all by herself, and then how lonely she was! Her only diversion was to stare at the screen that covered one of the six sides of the room, where she could see colored scenes that appeared to have three dimensions. In other ways, also, the pictures were not like Earthly television; one difference was that the scene always contained the same underground gallery, shining in a purplish light, and supported by seven-branched pillars of translucent blue. Along this gallery from time to time lizard forms could be seen dragging themselves, sometimes with wheezes and coughs that Eileen could not hear but could plainly see, and sometimes so sick that they had to be supported by their fellows. These scenes, Eileen concluded, were recorded by automatic photography and were transmitted by wire, so that they kept flashing before her in the mechanical way of a blinker system.

Soon she had become very tired of the sameness of the lizard processions. If she had had anything better to do, she would not have given them a glance. Oh, when, when would Xuxto let her out of this miserable prison? When, when would Ted find out where she was and come to her rescue?

She had almost despaired when one day her hopes were fanned back to life. She had been seated cross-legged on the floor, glancing indifferently at the screen. All at once, something unusual caught her eye. Along the gallery beneath the seven-branched pillars, six big Drumgradians were moving more purposefully than any she had seen for a long time; unlike most, they did not seem sick at all. They held great sticks and spears in their clawed hands, their eyes flamed with changing colors, and their scales flashed from cherry red to pumpkin-orange, jade-green, and lemon-yellow. "What are they about?" she wondered.

And then she saw the smaller, copper-tinted Drumgradian with amber-hued front eyes. And just beside him she recognized a familiar round red pug-nosed face. "Heavens!" she cried. "Chief Callahan!"

Even as these words escaped her lips, two other figures swept into view. The first had a greyhound face and small searching eyes deep-set beneath bushy brows. And the other—at the sight of his tall form, black hair, and bespectacled black eyes, she shrieked, and almost fell. "Ted!" she screamed.

Over and over again, at the top of her voice, she called to him, forgetting that he could not see or hear her. "Ted, hear I am! Oh, Ted, come and save me!"

But the three men, along with the Drumgradians, strode out of sight and did not come back. And the slow hours still went by, while the girl ranged the floor in feverish expectation and her heart pounded furiously. Whenever she heard footsteps approaching, her hopes rose almost unbearably; but an icy disappointment would seize her when Xuxto entered on one of her frequent visits. After all, had she only dreamed that she had seen the men?

There were moments when she almost thought so, while she scanned the colored pictures on the screen, hoping against hope for another sight of Ted. "Why doesn't he come? Why doesn't he come?" she wept over and over again. "Dear God, why doesn't he come?"

But still there was no answer.

In an immense, vaulted, purple-roofed hall, beneath the shimmering rainbow tints of the faintly illuminated walls, the Trivate Olero half reclined on his great raised couch. The orange front eyes and the copper-tinted rear eyes of the ruler shone with a flickering brilliance, and his tail-eye blinked red and blue. Colored flashes, likewise, issued from his huge writhing and twisting tentacles, though the sparks were fewer than of old, and did not change in hue quite so swiftly. His tentacles, even larger than normal, displayed bluish and blood-red swellings near the base. Now and then he lunged forward, and sneezed.

Around the couch several attendants stood in waiting, also sneezing in the chilly air forced in through the several big faucet-shaped blowers recently installed at one end of the hall. Obsequiously the attendants touched their tails to the floor and held out their clawed hands in homage.

Meanwhile, in an anteroom, two Drumgradians stood glancing in at the Trivate and muttering among themselves.

"By my scales, Orneppu," said the smaller of the pair, "our good Olero is almost back to himself."

"Yes, Mervex—and so much the worse for us!" grumbled the other, giving a flap to his long, flat, silver-scaled tail. "The gods of the three moons will testify, I never had it so easy as when the Trivate could send no tentacle messages."

"Nor I, Orneppu. What a strange, pleasant feeling, to do as I wish without always hearing somone snapping I did wrong! You know, this taste of freedom, Orneppu, makes me wonder. Must we go on for thousands, thousands of days—"

He halted, silenced by the warning flashes at the tips of Orneppu's tentacles. But the two creatures eyed one another with knowing glints of their glittering front eyes.

Minutes later, they were drawn into the main hall by the sight of a slim young Drumgradian who had come hopping in and flung himself down on the inlaid floor beside the Trivate.

From his squirming tentacles, a succession of varicolored sparks issued, and were answered by a sputtering of sparks from the Trivate, followed by a hoarse guttural speech.

"Gloto," he addressed his young subject, with a quick forward thrust of his enormous wedge-shaped head, "I am still not quite well, though thanks to the cold-air treatment prescribed by our able Zyreppoqs, I am much better. My tentacles are working again, but it still hurts me to use them. So, for the time, we must speak by the crude primitive word method. What was it that you wanted to tell me, Gloto?"

"O glorious, O noble Master," Gloto began, while his swaying tail brushed the floor, "we have just had news—dreadful news. We tried to send you word by tentacle flashes, but you seemed not to hear."

The Trivate's orange front eyes shone balefully. His huge mouth, opening as if to snap at someone, revealed the cavernous scarlet interior. "What is the news?" he demanded.

"O magnificent Leader, I hesitate to profane the sanctity of your presence, but must mention the vilest of words. The Narg, O enlightened—"

"What about the—the—no, I will not speak the accursed name!" sputtered the Trivate, between sneezes. "What about that pit of iniquity? Have those beasts committed new crimes?"

"Yes, O majestic Prince! The convicts have had the audacity to revolt. So have the guards and other Nargites, under the leadership of three of those low two-eyed animals from outer space—"

"What!" roared the Trivate, lunging forward so sharply that the watchers feared he would fall off his couch. "Did I not order them all *Thranku?*"

"Truly, O far-seeing Lord. But they have a *Nujeema,* whose wonders have saved them. They have broken out of the Narg in a great mob, and invaded the respectable districts. They have passed the Wall of Rock and the Wall of the Sword-Leaves. Now only the Moat of the Black Monster and the Wall of the

Speared Top keep them from your consecrated realm."

The Trivate growled like a car-engine in distress, and his tentacles let out sparks. His front eyes turned from orange to scarlet; the green of his scales gave way to purple-red. His tail thumped angrily against the rear of his couch.

"Where were my guards when this happened?" he howled. "We will find out! I will order an investigation! The guilty ones will curse the eggs that hatched them! Meanwhile, those vermin of Nargites and their scaleless leaders must be wiped out!"

"But, resplendent Ruler, as I have told you, they are already at the Wall of the Speared Top—"

"What of it?" bawled Olero, his scales resuming their normal green. "Thanks to the cleverness of my engineers, the Wall of the Speared Top is impossible to pass!"

"Yes, august Sovereign, but just the same we fear—"

Before Gloto could finish, a commotion broke out amid the purplish mists at a far end of the hall, and a creature sprang forward, panting heavily. He was big and gray-scaled, and waved his tentacles frenziedly as he dashed to the base of the Trivate's couch, threw himself to the floor, and stretched his long tail behind him in obeisance.

"O Center of Light! O superb—" he began, breathlessly. "There is more news—more news!"

"More news, Bolunk?" demanded Olero, examining the newcomer by turns with his orange front eyes, his coppery rear eyes, and his blinking tail-eye. "Good news?"

"Bad news, O eminent Seer! Those tailless brutes, accompanied by some armed traitors from the—pardon the word, O luminous Sage—some armed traitors from the Narg—they have found their way to the under-passages beneath the Wall of the Speared Top, and are even now on their way here!"

The Trivate sat up erect, coughed once or twice, then fell back on his couch with a rumbling of laughter.

"How many of them are there?"

"We are not sure. Maybe thirty or forty, O distinguished—"

Olero's laughter became louder. He rocked back and forth on his couch, and amusement glittered in his orange front eyes.

"Thirty or forty? Ho, ho, ho! You mean to say, thirty or forty rebels think to attack the great ruler of Arvandu? Never, in all my thousands of days, have I heard of anything so absurd! We will brush them off like specks of dust!"

"Of course, all-knowing Chieftain!"

"First I will play with them. I will lead them on. Then I will strike—and by the gods of the three moons, they will curse their own defiance!" the Trivate went on, his tail waving with satisfaction as he contemplated his revenge. Then eagerly he called, "Mottil! Ottro!" And he bent down, and engaged in a long whispered conference with two henchmen, while his tentacles waved and his tail-eye blinked red and blue.

CHAPTER XIV

In single file the three men and the six Drumgradians followed Glyp through tunnels so low-roofed that they had to crawl, and so narrow that they could barely squeeze through.

"By gum, it's worse than a coal mine!" grumbled Callahan, whose bulky form had great difficulty in negotiating the twists and turns.

"What worries me," muttered Harwood, feeling warily for his way as they wound through almost total darkness, "is that if any of these beasts of Drumgradians should get wind of where we are—"

He paused, seeing no need to finish the sentence.

"These are old, almost forgotten passageways," explained Glyp. "In the old days they were used by secret agents of the Trivate, but are now abandoned. The entrances on the Trivate's side, however, may be guarded."

His fears turned out to be well founded. Suddenly the tunnel shot up into a wider, purple-lighted gallery, where a black-striped Drumgradian stood with a long, jagged-edged spear. Glyp, who was in the lead, instantly started back, and motioned his comrades to silence. "We'll take a detour," he whispered, and found his way by touch through another long, blind passageway, in which Callahan got stuck and had to be jarred loose by his companions, while rocks rattled down ominously from the ceiling. Finally, after endless agonies, they saw a faint purplish glow ahead, and Glyp, creeping forward to reconnoiter, started into a wider corridor with a cry of relief.

Sprawled in the middle of the gallery, flat on his back, lay a black-striped Drumgradian, his spear beside him on the floor. He was breathing heavily but otherwise barely moved except when now and then his chest was racked with coughing. There was a dull glow in his eyes, and he gave no sign of noticing the newcomers.

"Now at last we've passed under the Wall of the Speared Top!" reported Glyp, twisting his tail in high satisfaction as they hurried on. "By my five eyes! it's cold down here!"

Truly, by native standards, it *was* cold—down somewhere in the sixties. But the three men rejoiced in the refreshing coolness, which, they knew, was Drumgrade's way of meeting the epidemic of colds.

"It's not far now to Olero's palace," Glyp cautioned, in tones that his hearers had trouble to follow. "Go very quietly. Watch out for the Trivate's guards."

But as they trooped along, three abreast, they saw no Drumgradians at all except several who lay about helplessly sick. This, however, did not reassure them. "You know, it's suspicious," Harwood whispered, as his keen eyes ran up and down the vaulted, purple-lighted tunnel. "It's just like they were laying low, waiting for us to walk into a trap."

"I've had the same feeling," admitted Ted. There was a disturbing silence about those weird passageways; he could imagine that unseen eyes were peeping out at him at every turn. Besides, he was beginning to wonder whether Glyp and his small band were not, after all, attempting a lunatic thing.

In a little while, the corridor split into two. To their right, another gallery reached in a blaze of amethyst, its high ceiling like an inverted V. "This is the way!" said Glyp.

He had barely reached the junction point when a blinding white flash, accompanied by a crash of thunder, streaked just in front of his face. As he leapt back in alarm, other flashes zigzagged like lightning, while the thunder continued and grew even louder. His tentacles waving vehemently, he motioned the small company away.

"It's something they've installed only recently, while I was away," he explained apologetically. "Surely, the gods of the three moons are with us, else we would not have escaped. So have no fear, my friends. I know another way into the palace."

Now his followers moved more warily than ever, scarcely daring to speak as they stole after him through long branching underground passages, where they had to crawl again on hands and knees. Several times Glyp seemed baffled. "May the imps of the deep craters curse them!" he growled, as he paused at the brink of a dim precipice and began wearily retracing his footsteps. Then they were balked by a swishing stream, which they could hear but not see, and more than once they had to retrace their steps. By this time the men were tired, thirsty, and hungry.

It was much later when Glyp paused, bewildered. In the darkness, the others could not see his face, but they observed the reddish sparks that shot out of his tentacles. "I—I think I've lost my way," he confessed.

Ted groaned, and Harwood cursed beneath his breath. The six Drumgradian guards all banged their tails angrily against the pavement, and began edging away; Ted thought that they were about to desert. It reassured him only slightly to reflect that they had nowhere to go.

"By my scales, we'll start away somewhere! Somehow I'll get my bearings," Glyp decided, as he set off down a purple-lighted gallery that looked exactly like scores of others. For a while he was silent. But after a few hundred yards, he became cheerful again. "Ah, I told you! The gods of the three moons are with us!" he rejoiced, pointing to a gallery lighted with an apple-green glow. "Unless the imps of the craters deceive me again, this leads straight to the palace!"

As the apple-green gallery was exceptionally wide, he moved close to the right-hand wall, so that his nine companions might take their places beside him. It was his position near the wall that saved him in the ensuing emergency.

Like a blast of machine-guns, a loud rattling, whirring, and clattering burst forth. At the same time, the three men and the six guards cried out in pain and terror. Around their knees, around their waists and arms, coils of thin wire had wound from apertures suddenly opened in the floor, catching them as in strait-jackets. Barely able to move, the men groaned and writhed, but the more they struggled to free themselves, the more the wires cut into their skins. The Drumgradians were less vulnerable, since the wires could not penetrate their scales; but they were clamped down until no part of them could move except their wildly twisting tentacles. Only Glyp, being just out of reach of the wires, had been more fortunate.

With a rapid tail-flick, he had brushed away a few thin entangling wires; then, with a spring-like movement as of a dog who scents danger, he had leapt aside. By a bare inch, he had saved himself.

"Scales of the Trivate! this is a sorry mess," he ruminated, as he heard the oaths, growls, and curses of his nine companions while they struggled like creatures engulfed in quicksands. "It's a new invention since my time."

Nevertheless, the cries for help seemed not to move Glyp as he coolly and speculatively surveyed the captives.

"What are you waiting for? Why don't you come and free us?" shouted Ted, as he wrestled with the wires, while visions came to him of the frantically buzzing insects which, in his childhood, he had seen trapped on sticky fly-paper.

Glyp still stood regarding the victims quizzically. His tentacles squirmed and his head twisted from side to side. But he made no move to help them.

"By the blue stars of the north, what can I do?" he answered, quietly. "If I too were caught, then in all our great city of Arvandu, there would be no power to help any of us."

Ted, remembering the Trivate's spear-wielding guards, knew that Glyp spoke the truth. If only he were not so matter-of-fact!

"There is just one slight chance," Glyp went on, ignoring the torrent of pleas that still rang out in Drumgradian. "I will go for help."

"But where? How? As you prize your own life, don't desert us!" begged Ted, as Glyp began to withdraw.

"I will do as the gods of the three moons permit. Am I too not in danger here so near Olero's palace?" Glyp demanded, with his first show of emotion, as the distance between him and his comrades widened. "If I can—I will be back. If not—you will know that the Trivate has me."

With this chilly assurance, he wheeled about. A moment later his copper-hued form, with a furiously blinking tail-eye, had disappeared around a turn in the gallery.

Meanwhile the captives, squirming and twisting less energetically, well knew the futility of resistance. For a long while no one spoke. "Well, by God," Callahan finally broke the silence, "that sure is a good one on us. I'll have to remember it when we get back on Earth. As a new way of catching bank robbers—"

"Sure, Chief, you can patent it and make your fortune," came Harwood's answer, in an ironic drawl. "That is, *when* you get back on Earth."

"Well, no use looking on the dark side of things," argued Ted, trying hard to keep down his mounting despair. "I have confidence in Glyp. I'm sure he'll do something."

"Yes, most likely His Highness the dictator will get down on his knees before him!" mocked Harwood, with bitter pessimism. "What's the use of kidding ourselves? How can a rogue like that help us? Can't you see, his only interest is in saving his own skin—I mean, his own damned scales!"

Logically, of course, Harwood was right. And yet somehow, deep down, Ted felt that Glyp would not forsake them. This, it was true, became increasingly hard to believe as time went by, time that seemed endless, infinite, while the men stood like trapped foxes and the wires bit ever more deeply into their flesh, and they grew hungrier, thirstier, and wearier, and the apple-green gallery light looked down on them steadily, coolly, pitilessly. At every slight sound, they started anxiously, looking with leaping pulses for Glyp's return, but knowing that they were more likely to see the black-striped, spear-wielding guards of the Trivate.

In a small, purple-walled room, Orneppu moved about slowly, his scaled body glittering with a shimmery silver, his tentacles flashing sparks with a rhythm as of telegraphic signals. Then suddenly the sparks ceased.

"It is as we feared, Mervex," he sighed to the smaller companion who, with orange-spotted gray scales and a tail-eye that flickered deep-yellow, stood solemnly opposite him.

"Yes, it is all as we feared. The Trivate—may his scales wither and fall off!—is well enough again to send out his messages. Everything now will be as in the old times. All our remaining thousands of days we will have to serve him, tied from tail to tentacle."

"Truly!" groaned Mervex. "The gods of the three moons, Orneppu, have shown us no way to save ourselves—" He broke short; then, in a changed tone, warned, "Listen!"

A faint threshing, as of a tail swishing along a pavement, could be heard from outside.

Hastily Orneppu turned to a tiny peephole in the wall. Then, with a cry of astonishment, he threw open a bottle-shaped door.

"Glyp!"

"Zuzum!"

Immediately Orneppu and the newcomer embraced, their tails tangling and intertangling affectionately, while their tentacles gave out sparks.

"As I love my scales, Glyp, how can it be?" Orneppu demanded, when the greetings were over. "Tell me all about it, old friend. You need not fear to speak before Mervex here. He is one of us."

"I am one of you," testified Mervex. "Surely, you remember me from the old days?"

"But you, Glyp, you were sentenced to the Narg," Orneppu hastened on. "Have you forgotten the penalty, if you escape and are caught?"

He drew seven claws significantly across his throat.

"I have not forgotten. But life in the Narg was not life at all. When I risk it—what do I really risk?"

"Life here is nothing, either," Mervex grumbled.

Turning toward the other two with a vigorous swing of his tail, Glyp hastened on, in a screeching voice, "That is why I am here, Zuzum. The prisoners in the Narg—they are rebelling, aided by those queer Earthlings, one of whom is a *Nujeema*. Now we are all in trouble. I have come to ask your aid."

Drawing close to one another, the three Drumgradians conferred in lowered tones. And while from time to time they glanced warily out through the peepholes, a new excitement came into their voices, their tail-eyes sparkled, and their front-eyes flashed with ever-changing colored glints.

By twisting and squirming, the men had slightly eased the pressure on their cramped muscles. But otherwise there had been little change, except that the pain in their limbs gradually grew harder and harder to bear. How long would the torture last? All that they knew was that already it had dragged out for hours.

"Well, it's nice and ironic, when you come to think of it," Harwood reflected wryly. "Here we've come this tremendous distance, the first men in all history to journey nearly a thousand light-years, only to end up in this silly way—trapped like skunks by some foul lizard monsters!"

"Now, now, George, you're going just a little ahead of yourself," protested Callahan, whose normally red face had turned white. "We sure ain't ended yet!"

"Not by a million miles!" chimed in Ted, still battling to hold up his hopes. "Maybe I'm crazy to say this, but somehow I have faith we'll come through." Even as he spoke, his thoughts were traveling to Eileen, who, wherever she was, might have the good luck not to be caught like a snared rabbit.

But he was not reassured as his gaze fell upon the captive Drumgradians, who stood stolid, unmoving, their eyes dull and listless, like creatures stoically resigned.

Was it part of the diabolical plan to keep them trapped here indefinitely, protracting their agonies? He half believed so. Since escape was impossible, the enemy had no need to hurry. Like the spider who has wrapped the struggling fly in its coils, the torturer could leave the feast to be devoured at leisure. Worse still! being able to make themselves invisible, the monsters might be standing over them even now.

Still deep in such broodings, Ted was startled by a clattering from just beneath him. The noise was not loud, but his heart leapt violently. He heard gasps from the other men, and glanced anxiously down the apple-green hall. "This is *it!*" he told himself. Then he heard another clattering, and, miraculously, the wires unwound from his limbs. He was free!

Painfully he moved his muscles, which were so cramped that at first he could hardly manage them. At the same time he observed that the other men, with oaths and mumblings of relief, were also free, as were the six Drumgradians.

"Lord! Lord! Am I dreaming?" he heard his own voice, somehow strange and unreal. And then, seeming equally unreal and strange, a threshing and thumping sounded behind him, and he swung about to see eight Drumgradians drawing near, and cried out in instant recognition.

Near the head of the approaching company, he saw Glyp, his amber front eyes shining brightly; at his side were the silver-scaled form of Orneppu and Mervex's orange-spotted shape. The other five were ordinary-looking Drumgradians whom Ted did not recognize, though two of them had the long curved spears and the silver badges of guards.

"Friends, have no fear!" Glyp called out, as he hopped forward. "Orneppu and Mervex—I have brought them to join us. And they—they have persuaded some of their brothers, who have served in the palace of the Trivate."

"Truly, we have been too long under Olero's tail!" grumbled one of the creatures, as he drew near.

"For thousands of days," growled another, "we have been waiting for our chance!"

"But how, how could you free us so suddenly?" Ted inquired of Orneppu, who had greeted him like an old friend.

"Oh, that, she was simple," replied Orneppu, in his choicest English. "My brother Kayfu here"—he pointed to a large Drumgradian with a red-mottled bluish tail—"he has the managing of the inner defendings. All he had to do was to turn a—what do you call it?—a switch."

Meanwhile, all the newly arrived Drumgradians were threshing about in high excitement.

"They are very eager, but we must act fast," Glyp hastily confided to Ted, after passing out some capsules of food and vials of drink, which did much to revive the men. "However, they do not like your plan to rush into the Trivate's palace, taking him by surprise—"

"That plan—she might have been wise when the Trivate's tentacles were still weak and he could send out no messagings," Orneppu explained. "But now his tentacles are getting strong again. Can you think what would happen if only a few of us tried to capture him?"

"Most likely there wouldn't be a shred left of us," concluded Ted grimly.

"He would send out messagings with his tentacles, and many would come rushing to his defendings. That would be our end. We would all be *Thranku*."

"Orneppu and I," stated Mervex, giving his tail an excited flip, "we have a better plotting."

"Much more better," affirmed Orneppu. "Do you forget all our brothers from the Narg, waiting outside the Wall of the Speared Top? If we bring them in, Olero's messagings will not matter. Our side will be so many, he can do nothing."

"But how can we get our followers here?" argued Ted. "Very few of them could come through those narrow deep tunnels. And the moat and the wall—how can they pass these?"

"Come with us! We will see!" snapped Orneppu.

His scales glittering like armor plate, and his tentacles giving out sparks, he started off down the apple-green gallery with Glyp and Mervex beside him, while the other Drumgradians and the three men followed in an enthusiastic company.

CHAPTER XV

Back and forth, back and forth beside the Moat of the Black Monster, the rebels pushed and squirmed, waving their great flat lizard tails, and twisting their tentacles into curls and spirals. Across from them, the Wall of the Speared Top arose, sullen and beetling, spiked and polished and as inaccessible as ever, though scores of throats still screeched defiance. "Down with the Trivate! Forward, forward for the rights of plain Drumgradians!"

But a change had come over the rioters. Some of them lay flat on the stone pavements, coughing and sneezing; others moped about listlessly, or staggered as if ready to collapse. Many, however, still paraded with triumphant shouts, displaying the glittering loot of the bubble-like palaces, while the smoke of bonfires and of blazing buildings darkened the sky.

Meanwhile at one side, in the court of a shimmering W-shaped dwelling, Kryku and his two chief aides stood conferring.

"As I value my tail, brothers," he was saying, "it is long, very long since the *Nujeema* left along with Glyp and the others. Why do they not return?"

"Why not? Yes, why not?" echoed Quenaquak, a dull reddish smolder in his front eyes. "I fear that the gods of the three moons have forsaken us."

"That cannot be!" denied Dracu, bringing his seven-clawed hands together with an emphatic clattering. "They would never leave us to fall again beneath the tail of Olero!"

"But our followers—they groan from this dread new weakness," Kryku remarked, giving his black-striped gray form an uneasy toss. "More and more of them drop out, and are of no more help to us than if they were never hatched. But this, brothers, is not the worst. Have you not noticed how some of them creep away back to their homes in the Narg?"

"Truly, I counted five such today," snorted Quenaquak, his tentacles sparkling angrily.

"Even now, enough are left," answered Kryku, pointing to the swarms still threshing about with stones and sticks. "But if the *Nujeema* and Glyp stay away much longer, others will desert, and others and still others, until we will be all alone. What then will we do against the hosts of the Trivate?"

His comrades did not answer. Every light went out of their front eyes, their rear eyes, and their tail-eyes. "What will we do against the hosts of the Trivate?" repeated Kryku. "How will we fight against his strong claws?"

Before them stretched the waters of the moat, dark, stagnant, and scum-covered as ever. Opposite them loomed the glistening, bottle-green, unbroken sheet of the wall, marked on top by projecting towers and dagger-edged spikes. But of Ted and Glyp and their companions there was still no sign.

"A partitioning of the Wall of the Speared Top, Earthling, she can be opened to let a road through. Also, a bridge from the wall to cross the Moat of the Black Monster."

"I know that, Orneppu," acknowledged Ted, as he and the other two men left the apple-green gallery along with their Drumgradian attendants, and started down one of the familiar purple-lighted corridors. "We came across the bridge and through the wall when we went to see Olero. But how can our comrades outside get through now?"

Orneppu rattled the seven claws of one hand across the silvery scales of his breast, and his voice was down almost to a whisper.

"I have given much thought to that, Earthling. We must get around the Red Guardian of the Wall."

"What's the Red Guardian of the Wall?"

Orneppu's sparkling tail-eye showed his agitation. "One of the Trivate's picked and trusted, what do you call them?—followers. The Guardian has a place of honor, and boasts that he never sleeps. He regulations the only way through the wall and over the moat. But maybe he has fallen down with the coughing weakness."

"What if he has not the weakness, or has recovered?"

Orneppu growled beneath his breath. "In that case—may the gods of the three moons help us! But we shall see, Earthling. We shall see."

For a long distance they kept on in silence, until at last the gallery slanted upward into the open and they found themselves in a blaze of sunlight, on a street bordered on the right by pearly mansions shaped like huge inverted turnips, and on the left by impenetrable hedges of plants with long blue-green leaves out-turned like saw-edges. Ahead of them, less than a quarter of a mile away, they saw the glistening bottle-green mass of the Wall of the Speared Top, and noted with satisfaction that they were inside this forbidding boundary.

A few hundred yards from the wall, Orneppu paused. "Mervex, Glyp and I will go on," he decided, pointing to a lane which led out of sight between the wall and a hedge of the blue-green plants. "The Red Guardian, his stationing is just beyond. Maybe, since he knows us very long, he will listen to us. The rest of you stay here till we come back."

Mervex, Glyp, and Orneppu had already started away, when the latter turned back suddenly, lifting the long claws of one hand in a gesture of caution. "Earthlings," he warned, "no matter what happens, stay here till we come back! Do not, as you value your lives, look to see what we are doing!"

"As we value our lives, we will not look," promised Ted.

"You are now in a—what is your name for it?—a dead-end street in a far-out district, and no one will be passing," stated Orneppu.

A long interval went by while the three men and the Drumgradians waited and Orneppu and his two comrades interviewed the Red Guardian of the Wall.

This official did not belie his name. He was exceptionally large, more than seven feet tall, and blazed with red from the top of his wedge-shaped head to the tip of his long flat tail. His front eyes, by contrast, were of a glowing black; his rear eyes were of a sultry, sulphurous yellow, and his tail-eye blinked blue, green, and orange in a series of irregular sparkles. In his extraordinarily long clawed left hand, he held a five-pointed spear taller than himself.

Orneppu, Glyp, and Mervex, as they approached, hailed him with cries of fellowship, and the three briefly touched tails in greeting.

"It is long, brothers, since I have seen you," said the Guardian, with a friendly swaying of his tentacles toward Mervex and Orneppu, while he stood back to the wall. "As I love the Trivate, I swear it grows monotonous, standing here all day, every day, seeing no one. Tell me, what is the news?"

Orneppu clapped his claws together, and passed many minutes in regaling the Red Guardian with anecdotes of recent happenings, while all joined in howls of laughter. Only after a long wait did Orneppu approach a more important subject.

"Have you heard, brother," he asked, cautiously, "of the outbreak in the Narg?"

"Yes, by the gods of the three moons! But not in a million days can that scum pass the moat and the wall!"

"Not in a million million days!" agreed Mervex. "That is, not unless someone lets them through."

The black of the Guardian's front eyes had given way to a baleful scarlet. "And who," he screeched, "would let those vermin through?"

"Not you. And not I," said Orneppu. "But the land is filled with traitors."

"Let any rogues try! My tail! Just let them try!" bellowed the Guardian, swinging his five-pointed spear to show how he would dispose of any assailants. "I will throw all such trash to the Black Monster of the Moat!"

On and on he went, growing still louder in reciting the dire penalties that awaited all violators of the wall. His voice, rising to a thunder-pitch, could be heard by the three men standing just beyond a turn in the lane.

"Good Lord! Sounds like somebody's fighting the Civil War!" muttered Callahan.

Ted, in his excitement and his concern for Orneppu, had forgotten the warning not to show himself. On an impulse, he shot around a corner of the hedge, and found himself looking at a huge red Drumgradian, who stared at him not fifty feet away.

The Red Guardian, in the midst of depicting various exquisite torments of rebels, stopped short as if he had seen a ghost. After a startled second, while Ted slipped hastily out of sight, his voice became even louder than before.

"My claws! Did you see that? One of those hideous two-eyed beasts! those scaleless Earth-animals whom our great Olero has ordered to be *Thranku!* Now I must send the good Trivate a message, so that he may know the brute has escaped, and rush guards to capture and destroy him!"

From the tips of the Red Guardian's tentacles, sparks flashed in bewildering colors. In his preoccupation, he did not see how, even while the sparks flickered and his tail-eye swung far forward in his zeal, Glyp stole behind him, deftly threw open a panel in the wall, pulled a lever, and shut the panel again. Nor did the Guardian know how, at the wall's opposite side, a bridge unfolded across the moat and a partition in the wall drew aside, revealing a wide roadway that passed through the wall and connected with the bridge.

CHAPTER XVI

"No power in all Drumgrade, Earthlings, can save you if the Trivate catches you now!"

So Orneppu warned in a subdued voice, as he and the small party of Drumgradians started swiftly away with the three men along the base of the wall.

Ted and his comrades needed no reminder. They well realized that Olero's rage would know no limits now that he had found that his commands had not been executed. They also knew that he would spare no effort to recapture the fugitives.

Their only hope, therefore, lay in the rebellious Nargites. But even though Glyp had opened the way across the moat and through the wall, might not Kryku and the other leaders hold back, seeing in the opening of the wall a possible ruse to entrap them? And even if they did pass through, how would they know of the Earth-men's plight? Would they come in time to save them?

"Well, we've beat them devils lots of times already," remarked Callahan, feeling for reassurance at the muscles of his flexed right arm. "You can just bet we'll put it all over them again."

"Me—I wouldn't bet a bogus dollar bill, if I had

one," answered Harwood, with a wry grimace. "Don't you see, that whole scaly police force'll be out after us now!"

"This way! Down this way!" Orneppu directed, turning into a lane bordered on both sides by the saw-leafed plants. But suddenly he halted, and let out a sharp cry. "Back!" With one clawed hand, he was pointing to a waving spear which had flashed into view ahead of them around a bend in the lane.

As they rushed back, turning into a street to the left between two rows of Y-shaped dwellings fronted with a white metal that looked like aluminum, Mervex uttered a shout. Projecting above a blue-green fence of leaves while approaching at a steady pace, the tips of several spears swung before them.

But Glyp, remembering a path that wound roughly parallel to the wall amid a jungle of saw-leaves, temporarily saved the fugitives. As they looped along at a panicky speed, they could hear a harsh clamor of voices, and knew that they were being pursued if not surrounded, and might be confronted at any moment by a wall of spear-wielding guards.

But vaguely, from the distance, they heard another clamor, a hoarse continual roaring of voices—and their pulses leapt with new hope. "Can it be? Oh, can it be?" they asked, turning to one another doubtfully. "Is it possible?"

But even as they put this question, they noticed with dismay how their little company had shrunken. All the Drumgradians, except Orneppu, Mervex, and Glyp, had deserted them.

"Well, we can't blame the rascals for wanting to save their own hides—or, rather, their own scales," Ted reflected; then gasped, and felt that all was lost.

In the street before him, a trapdoor had rattled open, and the first of a squad of spear-bearing Drumgradians burst into view.

"Back! Back! Back!" Orneppu again shouted. But it was too late. The foremost of the newcomers, a red-banded huge black beast, had dashed forward, pointing to the Earth-men with one long arm. "I have orders from our great and noble Trivate—" he began, while Ted wondered if it would be of any use to turn and run. But then surely they would be overtaken, even if they did not fly straight into the claws of fresh enemies.

"Orders from our great and noble Trivate! Orders to take the foreign beasts dead or alive!" shrilled the red-banded beast, edging forward. And then, recognizing Orneppu and Mervex with surprise, "Brothers, what are you doing down here with these fiends from the sky?"

"They are not fiends, Mottil!" Orneppu pleaded. "As I have known you from of old, listen! These are new times. Do you not hear the rebels from the Narg?"

Mottil growled, and lunged toward Ted, who sprang back, barely out of reach. At the same time, the vague, hoarse uproar of voices was growing louder.

"If you harm so much as one claw of these Earthlings," Orneppu warned, "the Nargites will tear off your tentacles! They will throw you to the Black Beast of the Moat!"

"Do you not hear them? Listen! Do you not hear?" Mervex took up the cry, as the tumult of voices grew nearer.

The men could not catch the next words, which were spoken in Drumgradian, but they knew that

Orneppu and Mervex were heatedly arguing with the newcomers, and they realized that the aim was to gain time. This maneuver, however, seemed unavailing. Once more the red-banded monster raised his long arms to seize Ted, who had backed against a wall of saw-leaves, hardly knowing that they were cutting him.

"Mark me, brothers! As you value your tails, do you not hear?" Orneppu made his desperate last appeal.

The three men, straining their ears, heard no more than before. But the keener native senses made out the words, "Down with Olero! Down with Olero! Off with his tentacles! Forward, forward for the rights of plain Drumgradians!"

The tail-eyes of the red-banded one and his followers blinked uncertainly. Their front eyes and their rear eyes turned from yellow and green to a brooding crimson. Their clawed hands, raised for action only a moment before, fell hesitantly to their sides.

"Down with the Black Ones! Down with Olero! Pull his scales off! Forward, forward . . ." the cries resounded. And it was only moments later when the first of the mutineers burst into view from a side-lane, and started jubilantly toward Ted and his companions. *"Nujeema! Nujeema!* It is the *Nujeema,* who has worked wonders! He has thrown a bridge over the moat! He has made a way through the wall! *Nujeema! Nujeema! Nujeema!* May he live ten million days!"

In fierce resistance, Mottil and his followers swung their spears. But as well might they have wielded grass-blades. Their only possible course was to retreat, their tentacles sparkling as the mob poured toward them, first by the tens, then by the scores and hundreds.

"*Nujeema! Nujeema!* He has saved us! He has worked wonders! He has made a way through the wall! He has thrown a bridge over the moat!" the cries chorused forth, while the men had difficulty to avoid being crushed by the torrents of enthusiasts. Lifted on to the back of a seven-foot black-striped beast and carried forward in triumph while Callahan and Harwood were borne just behind him by other Drumgradians, Ted found himself entering a wide avenue lined with the shimmering bubble-like mansions. Solidly from side to side, this street was packed with his admirers, who, with tails threshing, tentacles waving, and eyes flashing every color from golden to scarlet and from electric blue to blazing white, continued to shout and yell, "*Nujeema! Nujeema!* He has saved us! He has worked wonders! He has made a way through the wall!"

And then, above all the other cries, there burst a still more tumultuous call, which rose to a thundering crescendo, "*Nujeema! Nujeema! Nujeema!* We will make him our new Trivate! The *Nujeema* will be our new Trivate! Our new Trivate! Our new Trivate! . . ."

Swarm after swarm, the Nargites streamed across the bridge and along the road under the wall. Hundreds of deserters, shouting and chanting, came flocking back; many, who had seeemed too sick to move, staggered to their feet and joined the exultant companies. Others, who had held aloof with various excuses, were swept along triumphantly with the invading throng. In a purple mist that gradually faded, the multitude spread out along the streets and avenues beneath the carrot-shaped and domed mansions, while a new cry stormed to their lips, "On to the Trivate's palace! On, on to the Trivate's palace! The Trivate's palace!" And mingled with this call, there came the repeated shout, "*Nujeema! Nujeema! Nujeema!* We will make him our new Trivate! Our new Trivate! *Nujeema! Nujeema!*"

"Well, how does it feel, old fellow, to be elected King of the Lizards?" Callahan threw out at Ted, as he clung to the back of a huge Drumgradian, who walked on all fours to support his weight. "As for me —by heck, man! I used to go horseback-riding, but I sure never expected to ride lizard-back!"

"If I were you," dourly answered Harwood, who was trying to get off the back of his immense carrier but was repeatedly poked back into place, "if I were you, I'd save my comments till this crazy ride was over —that is, if you're damned lucky enough to get out of it alive!"

"*Nujeema! Nujeema! Nujeema!* He has saved us! He has worked wonders! He will be our new Trivate! Down with Olero! Down with Olero!" the cries continued in an increasing din, while tails twisted and waved and tentacles flashed fire.

Then, as the commotion rose until it reminded the men of a gale-swept sea, they entered the Trivate's immense vaulted hall. Owing to the intervening crowd, they could not see the raised couch in the center, where the Trivate reigned in the midst of his attendants beneath the rainbow-tinted walls. But above all the other noises, they did hear screams, howls, bawlings, crashes, and clangings. Not until later were they told how the Trivate's bodyguard, vainly resisting, was overwhelmed by the invading host, trampled upon, bruised, mangled, and saved from instant death only by their thick colored scales.

Finally, after a prolonged pandemonium, a way was cleared and Ted was carried forward, while Harwood and Callahan were borne just behind him through the reverential crowds. *"Nujeema! Nujeema! Nujeema!"* applauded the mob. "Our new Trivate! Our new Trivate! May he live ten million days!"

But what had happened to the old Trivate? A moment later, the men could see for themselves.

Looming above the threshing hordes, and closely guarded by a row of spears, the green-scaled official stood in lordly dignity. His tail, swaying like an aroused cat's, blinked furiously red, green, and blue; his orange front eyes and coppery rear eyes blazed with steady brilliance; his writhing tentacles gave out streams of sparks. But as he turned from side to side, vainly seeking a way through the mob, he looked more and more like a wild beast at bay.

"Ottro! Mottil! Gloto!" he called, in a voice as shrill as a steam whistle, and swung his head in all directions, looking for his henchmen. But some, he knew, had been overpowered by the rebels; and of the others there was no sign.

"Ottro! Mottil! Gloto!" he shrieked over and over again. "Ottro! Mottil! Gloto! On the faith of our great city of Arvandu, help me! In the name of the gods of the three moons, avenge this sacrilege!"

There was more in the same vein, along with messages from his sparkling tentacles—all of which was possible only because of the awe in which he was still held by many, and their unwillingness to violate his sacred person. What he did not know was that scores of his followers, with shouts of "Down with Olero!" had already joined the revolutionists.

Now from the rabble a new cry arose. No one was ever able to say who started it, but it spread like a wind-whipped blaze, and was echoed and re-echoed with mounting enthusiasm by the entire crowd. "To the Narg with Olero! To the Narg with Olero! Lock him up in the Narg! In the prison of the Narg! Lock him up! Lock him up! To the Narg with Olero!"

These words, repeated in a fierce, echoing chant, had a hypnotic effect. "To the Narg with Olero! To the Narg with Olero! To the Narg, the Narg, the Narg with Olero!"

In a mighty wave, the multitude pushed toward the deposed dictator; like a twig they bore him along. Violently protesting, his tail beating frantically, his tail-eye blinking, his tentacles flashing more fiercely than ever, he called even above the bellowing of the crowd, "Ottro! Mottil! Gloto! Help me! Help me! For the love of the gods of the three moons, avenge this sacrilege!"

"To the Narg with Olero! Lock him up in the Narg! In the prison of the Narg! To the Narg with Olero! The Narg, the Narg, the Narg!" uproarious voices clamored, while Ted and his comrades had a last glimpse of Olero, his scales glittering a vivid green and his tentacles scintillating as he still towered above the billowing crowd and was shepherded out through a vaulted doorway beneath the shimmer of the many-tinted walls.

But new cries were resounding. "Hail, hail to the new Trivate! The *Nujeema! Nujeema!* All hail the new Trivate!"

Propelled by his admirers, half carried and half shoved, Ted found himself in the center of the hall, where he was lifted to Olero's long raised satiny purple couch.

"Our new Trivate! Our new and noble Trivate!" he heard his followers shouting. "*Nujeema! Nujeema!* May the gods of the three moons bless the *Nujeema!* May he live ten million days!"

Looking down at that solid, surging lizard mass, with their hosts of waving staves and clubs, Ted suddenly felt a chill. As the crowd still yelled and clamored, he could not understand most of their words. He did not know what was expected of him, or how their government was managed, or how he could possibly direct it; he only knew that the mob looked to him for wonders, and in his terror he almost wished to be safely back in the Narg. And as he stared at the beaming, red-faced Callahan and the ironically smiling Harwood, he wondered why the most dangerous of honors had fallen on him.

Just to his left, as he still listened to the reiterated cries, he was reassured to see the well-known silvery shape of Orneppu, his front eyes shining softly.

"Our new and noble Trivate! Our new and noble Trivate!" Orneppu addressed him, his tail flat along the ground in homage—and Ted was sure that he could detect an irony in his voice. "O great Leader, have you any orders?"

"Yes—an urgent one!" Ted surprised himself by answering. "One of our four Earth-people, Orneppu—the lovely one, with the long red hair and deep-blue eyes—I do not know where she is. See that she is found and brought to us—at once!"

"At once, O eminent Master—that is, if she has not been made *Thranku.*"

Orneppu swept the floor with his tail; retreated a few feet; and whispered to two large black-striped Drumgradians, who began hastily weaving their way out through the crowd.

CHAPTER XVII

With heavy tail-thumps, the black-striped callers rapped at a rose-hued, crescent-shaped door. For several minutes there was no answer, while the raps grew more insistent. Then a panel slid open, and two frightened eyes peeped out. "Name of the three gods, what is it?" a strident voice demanded.

"Open, Xuxto! We come at the order of our great and noble Trivate! Open! or face his vengeance."

Slowly the door swung on its hinges, and the two visitors passed into an immense, lavender-walled, octagonal room, where a six-legged crocodile-like creature ran about their knees with a long flapping tail, while several partly grown lizards screamed and fled.

"Xuxto," said one of the newcomers, severely, "the records show that a scaleless beast from outer space was assigned to you as a plaything for your young ones. Our great Trivate has ordered—"

Xuxto's convulsed face, her wildly waving tentacles and blinking tail-eye, betrayed her thoughts. Here were the Trivate's terrible followers again, come to take her Earthling, her dear Gi-gi, and make her *Thranku.*

"I—I—worshipful ones, I have no scaleless beast,"

she lied, while her normally pale yellowish complexion gave place to an agitated flame-color, and then to deep red. "She—she ran away long ago. We have not seen her since."

"We will look for her!"

Brushing Xuxto aside, the intruders ranged about the room, searching for evidences of side-doors and passageways, while the mistress continued to protest, "She is not here! As I value my claws, worshipful ones, I do not know where she went."

Having searched the room and several connecting chambers, one of the newcomers spied a stairway leading down.

"No, no, not that way!" pleaded Xuxto, placing herself in the searchers' path as they started to descend. "Down there—down there is a shrine, sacred to our family gods!"

The hysterical note in her voice only fanned the determination of her unwanted visitors. Down and down they wound, searching corridors and storerooms. Finally, however, their tails drooped with discouragement, and their dull, lusterless eyes bespoke their frustration.

"As I love my mother's scales! Do you not see?" Xuxto shrilled, in triumph. "There is nobody here!"

Growling, the searchers turned to leave. As a sign of his anger or perhaps as an outlet for his disappointment, one of them swung his tail with three resounding smacks against the stone pavement.

He could not have known that the noise would be heard by a girl lying in a small, windowless room beneath. Aroused from a sleep in which she had been with Ted in a blissful dream, she leapt to her feet in a delirium of hope.

"Ted! Ted!" she screamed, convinced that her dream was about to come true. "Ted! Ted! Here I am! Save me!"

As they started up the stairs, the two black-striped creatures stopped short. Their keen ears had caught the cries, though they did not understand the words. "By the three gods, who is that?" one of them demanded of Xuxto.

Her terrified silence was eloquent.

Within a minute, the searchers had forced from her the secret of the trapdoor, and one of them had made his way through the opening. Eileen, seeing the black-striped lizard form instead of her lover, shrieked and cowered against the wall. Nevertheless, she quickly realized that she had no choice but to go with the newcomers. Whatever happened, she decided, she would be brave. And whatever happened, it could not be worse than to be imprisoned in this wretched basement. Now, she was sure, she would never see Ted again. But if she must die, it would be with his name upon her lips.

As she dragged her way upstairs, with one Drumgradian in front of her and one behind, Xuxto ran frenziedly to the rear, shrilling, "Do not make her *Thranku!* Tell our great Trivate, do not make her *Thranku!* Do not make our Gi-gi *Thranku!*"

Surrounded by dozens of attendants, who never approached except with tails respectfully stretched flat along the floor, Ted tossed about uneasily on the raised couch of the Trivate, while Callahan and Harwood rested on smaller couches to his right and left. He was deep in a conversation with Orneppu and Mervex. "I don't want the others to know what we are saying," he had begun. "We must speak only in my own language."

"Of course, exalted Ruler," Orneppu had acknowledged, still with a note of irony.

Ted's voice, as he went on, had a deeply serious ring. "I know that it is a great honor. But it is too much of an honor. Is there any way to resign?"

Orneppu's tentacles gave out red, violet, and golden sparks. "No Trivate has ever—what is your word?—resigned. If he did, people would say he had forsaked the gods of the three moons. They would make him *Thranku.*"

"Being Trivate, then, is a life position?"

"A life position, O gracious Lord. That is, unless the people make revoltings against him, as they did with Olero."

Ted bit his lip, and was silent for a moment, then slowly went on, "I don't know a thing about making laws for your people—and sending out the messages they expect—"

"We will help you, O mighty Ruler," volunteered Mervex, with an eager turn of his orange-spotted gray body.

"We will be your ministers, O All-Powerful!" added Orneppu, his tail swaying and his tail-eye blinking. "Your messagings—you can send them through us. Our tentacles will flash them all over the city of Arvandu."

The thought shot across Ted's mind that, since he could not interpret the tentacle flashes, he would not know what orders Orneppu and Mervex were issuing. For all practical purposes, they would be the rulers. Yet he was thankful to have their aid. Without it, he would be helpless.

Cutting through his reflections, the voice of Callahan burst out cheerfully. "Well, old boy, now that you're the lord high mucki-muck, guess we'll have to get down on our knees before you. I expect you'll be giving us some new laws. Believe me, if I was in your shoes, there's one I'd put over darned fast."

"What's that?"

"A law against this straw and water they dish out to us. I'd see if I couldn't round up some real grub, like prime ribs or steak, or even some good old ham and eggs. And maybe throw in some beer, or a nice swig of Scotch or Bourbon."

"Well, I'll see what I can do," laughed Ted, then turned to the tall figure who lounged on the couch to his left, supported uncomfortably on one elbow. "And what law would you like, George?"

"Me?" answered Harwood, ruefully feeling at the thick beard that covered his once immaculately shaved face. "Well, if I were you, I'd make a law providing razors for all travelers from foreign planets. And also," he added, with a grimace of distaste at his formerly trim tweed suit, now soiled, shapeless, and threadbare, "I'd make it a capital offense not to provide clean new clothes for all visitors."

"Could stand a change myself," remarked Ted, noting that his own clothes, torn in several places and encrusted with dust, looked anything but royal. "But seriously, I've been wondering about that awful Narg—isn't there some way to abolish it—make it into a respectable district—"

"You've about as much chance of that, my boy," answered Harwood, drily, "as of teaching an elephant to hop. If they'd wanted to abolish the Narg, they'd have done it long ago."

Several Drumgradians, edging forward with tails flat along the floor, broke into the discussion with a variety of squeaks and screeches beyond Ted's fathoming. One of them, according to Orneppu, was presenting a petition to shorten claws. Another was forwarding a request to limit the thickness of scales. A third wanted the Wall of the Speared Top to be torn down. A fourth had a complaint against a neighbor, who, he alleged, caused confusion by giving out tentacle signals on the wrong wave-length. "Oh, good God," Ted groaned, "so this is what I'll have to listen to all the rest of my life!"

Meanwhile he kept looking hopefully about him for the return of the emissaries whom Orneppu had sent out to find Eileen. Why did they not come back? Surely, more than time enough had passed. But Orneppu, when queried, merely gave his tail a disdainful slap, and answered, "Have no fear, O honored Chief. They will find her—if she is not already *Thranku.*"

The long Drumgradian day was almost over, and Ted had left his couch to enter the *Olacho* or official private quarters of the Trivate, a sapphire-domed palace where he would pass the night in company with Harwood and Callahan, while twenty black-striped guards paced outside with blinking tail-eyes and several-pointed spears uplifted. Just as he reached the door of the rainbow-walled audience hall along with Orneppu, Mervex, and other attendants, he was startled to see two large striped Drumgradians approaching, and, just between them, a shrinking, woebegone figure that he recognized with a shock of joy.

"Eileen!" he shouted. And before the long-clawed hands of the guards could reach out to intervene, he and the girl were in each other's arms.

CHAPTER XVIII

"Sooner or later, O exalted Captain, there will be a great celebrating. You will take your oath by the gods of the three moons. Everybody will come to see you. You will make a long speech, which we will readify for you. It will be the most high honoring you can have."

Ted groaned. "Isn't there some way, Orneppu, to do without this honor?"

"No, O grand Trivate. The people—they expect it. However, we can wait many days, telling them you must look for the right sign from the three moons. Meanwhile, we can teach you to speechify better in Drumgradian."

This announcement, which crashed upon Ted's ears with the impact of a sentence in a criminal court, reinforced the desire which had been forming more and more in his mind, though he knew it to be the wildest of wild dreams. If only they could find some way back to Earth!

Both the other men had often expressed the same views. "I'd sure risk my right hand to be back in good old Plummetsville!" Callahan would remark. And Harwood would add, "Me—I'd risk my neck! Not that it's worth a cancelled postage stamp here in Drumgrade!"

But the most emphatic of all was Eileen. During the several days since her rescue, she had been assigned a guarded apartment near the Olacho, where she was far from happy. She could see Ted but a few minutes a day, since for more than seventeen hours he was expected to be on the official couch, where he listened to petitions that he seldom understood, while Orneppu and Mervex answered for him with speeches and tentacle flashes. "Oh, dearest," the girl would plead, when at the end of the long, wearying day he would seek her out during the brief period before the official *nucka* or slumber-time, "oh, dearest, will we ever get away from here? Can't we possibly go back to Earth?"

"Well, nine hundred light-years is a mighty long distance," he would answer, pressing her close. "Why can't we be married here?"

"Who would marry us? What kind of wedding would we have? And what would it mean, among a lot of lizards, who hardly leave us even a few minutes together?"

Impulsively she turned away, giving a disconsolate toss to her mop of red hair, which had grown long and unruly. Meanwhile Ted, hearing the droning signal of the *nucka,* had started sadly away. Ever since becoming Trivate, he reflected, he was even more tied by rules and less free than before.

"Is there any way for us Earth-people to get back to our own planet?" Ted asked Orneppu the next day.

The Drumgradian's front eyes blinked with a

succession of colors. "Why, O luminous Ruler," he demanded, "should you want to get back to your own planet? You are now in a positioning that most people would give their tails to have."

"We are homesick for our friends—our native land."

"Your friends, they are now the Drumgradians. Our city of Arvandu is your land."

Ted sighed, seeing no break in the walls around him.

"Couldn't you get us back to Earth if you wanted to?" he tried another tack.

"That, O eminent Lord, would give us no troubling. With anti-space and anti-time to serve us, it could be done as fast as a tail-flick. But why should you want to go?"

"Tell me this, my friend. Would you not like to be the Trivate in my place?"

Orneppu's color changed from silver to golden and yellow.

"O great Chieftain, you make—what you call it?—a big joking. Why should a poor humble Drumgradian be the Trivate?"

"You've done pretty well, Orneppu, as the Trivate's first assistant. Mervex could become your chief minister, maybe with Glyp beside him—"

In the deep reddish light that flamed from Orneppu's front eyes, Ted thought he could read awakening desire.

"What of our people?" asked the Drumgradian. "How can I tell them that their Trivate—their *Nujeema*—has gone?"

For a moment Ted was silent. "Well," he answered

at last, reflectively, "maybe I could sign a proclamation, saying I was called away—"

"Who would believe that?" Orneppu snorted. "They would say I tell bad stories, because I want to be Trivate. No, they must hear your own voice."

"I could make a speech, mentioning that I was going—"

"Then, O renowned Sovereign, do you think they would ever let you go?"

Ted bit his underlip ruefully. But a saving inspiration flashed over him. "What, Orneppu, if they hear my voice *after I am gone*—my voice, which they will recognize, telling them I must leave and they must honor you as their new Trivate."

"In that case, O Miracle Man, they would have to believe," conceded Orneppu, his tail swaying back and forth in rapid loops. "They would call you a more great *Nujeema* than ever."

"Also," added Mervex, who had been standing in the background silently listening, "we can say that you can make yourself unvisible, like us. Then they may think you are still here."

"I'll sure be invisible—nine hundred light-years away!" laughed Ted. And then, turning to Harwood, who had been reclining on his couch with a bored expression, "Looks to me, George, like you're going to be out one darned good tape recorder."

"If it will help us get away from this crazy planet," conceded Harwood drily, "it will be worth all the tape recorders that were ever made."

Immediately Ted began putting his plan into action. Telling the court attendants and waiting petitioners that he must hold a conference of state, he withdrew with Orneppu and Mervex into a secret anteroom, where he showed them how to operate the recorder. Both Drumgradians were quick in following instructions; after a test or two, they were able to thread the reel, play it, rewind it, and play it back. "It is a most great inventioning, O wise Leader," remarked Orneppu, admiringly. "In truth, you *are* a *Nujeema,* to have inventioned this wonder-machine."

"I am not the inventor," denied Ted. But the Drumgradians seemed not to hear him. "You are a *Nujeema,* a very great *Nujeema,* to make such a wonder-machine," they continued to applaud. And thus they gave birth to the legend that would ever afterwards be a shining part of Drumgradian lore.

Aided by Orneppu and Mervex, who filled in the gaps in his knowledge and supplied most of the words and phrases, Ted prepared what Harwood sarcastically termed his "farewell address" to the Drumgradians. No less than seven successive talks had to be recorded, the first six being erased before he made one which halfway pleased his instructors.

"Brothers of Drumgrade," his final version began, "I am called away by my duties as a *Nujeema,* but will be with you often when you cannot see me. Meanwhile I appoint my trusted minister Orneppu as Trivate in my place, and my able associates Mervex and Glyp as sub-Trivates. Obey them in all things. May the gods of the three moons pour blessings upon you! . . ."

There were several paragraphs more, repeating the same thought in different words. Mervex and Orneppu were fascinated. "No one could make imitationings of your voice, O revered Master," Orneppu stated. "With that quaint Earthling accent of yours, everybody will know it is you."

But Ted's thoughts were already on other matters. "Tell me, where is the spaceship *Great Galaxy?*" he asked, after the Trivate-to-be had received the recorder and the precious reel of tape.

"In the spaceport just outside the city, O great Commander. But to get into it," Orneppu added with a sly smile, "we need permissioning from the Trivate."

With a laugh, Ted gave the permission, after being assured that Orneppu and Mervex, having been trained in space navigation, could manage the ship without other crewmen.

"But you will have to be gone long," reasoned Ted. "Will the people not notice your absence?"

"We will not be gone long!" denied Orneppu. "Anti-time—she is no time at all!"

As the ship was fully equipped in the expectation of further voyages, few preparations were necessary. On the following night, when the long droning official signal had announced the slumber-time and the city had settled down for the eighteen-hour rest period, four scaleless and tailless adventurers stole off beside two tentacled lizard shapes. No one saw them gliding through the deserted streets beneath the carrot-shaped and bubble-like towers; no eye followed them as, by the light of two moons, they threaded the silence and crept into the sausage-shaped hulk of the *Great Galaxy.* Some time had to pass while the nagivators adjusted the controls; then there came the purring of atomic engines, a jolt—and Drumgrade lay beneath them.

"Will you have any trouble finding Earth?" Ted asked, just before he and his companions were lashed down with the silvery cords in preparation for anti-time and anti-space.

"Why any trouble, O mighty Lord? We set the dials to reverse our last flight—there is nowhere that we can go except to your planet. But I warn you," Orneppu amended, after a moment, "we cannot say where on Earth we will come down."

"Anywhere at all on Earth will be paradise." Eileen expressed the general thought.

A moment later, a glowing purplish patch of the wall had been stripped off, unbaring the red-plastic machine with its multitudes of knobs, sockets, and dials, and its perforations into which needle-like slits of metal were injected faster than the eye could follow. Once more a faint bluish mist surrounded the partitions; once more a nauseating chemical odor was in the air . . . then the travelers reeled, felt faint, and dropped into insensibility.

Above the coast of Tanganyika, three uncanny purplish flashes were observed one night by the startled inhabitants and reported by ships at sea. And out of the coastal brush of Tanganyika, on the following morning, four wanderers made their way to a village, where the natives were astonished to see three ragged-bearded and bedraggled men and a slim girl with untended long red hair and deep-blue flaming eyes. At a trading post where tramp steamers occasionally called, the four obtained a passage to Bombay, the men arranging to work as deckhands to pay their way and that of their lady companion. Having reached the Indian seaport, they went to the American Consul, who at first could not take their claims seriously. But a cable sent in code to the celebrated detective agency, Harwood Associates, Inc., of New York, evoked a surprising response—established that one of the dishevelled strangers was none other than George Orson Harwood, whose disappearance the previous June had created a worldwide sensation. Events now moved rapidly; and though few could accept the adventurers' fantastic story, funds for their passage home were forthcoming.

Thus it came about that the four travelers, arrayed in clean new clothes, stood together one January evening on the deck of a steamer cleaving the calm immensities of the Indian Ocean. For a long while they stared in silence into the star-flecked, moonless night.

"It's almost incredible," said one of them, a tall, dark youth, "but the calendar shows we were away only a little more than six months."

"According to my calculations, Ted," answered a lean man with a greyhound face, "that's just the period we passed on Drumgrade. It's hard to believe this stuff about anti-time, but how else would you account for our being only half a year older?"

"Me—I feel a hundred years older," remarked a red-faced, pug-nosed man. "By glory, every day on Drumgrade seemed a month long. I still see them five-eyed reptiles in my nightmares."

Meanwhile, the one woman in the party, gazing intently into the bright stars of the tropical night, pointed vaguely to the northern skies.

"Somewhere over there—far out over there," she remarked, "is that weird planet, and all its lizard people."

"Yes, and one of the strange things, dearest," declared the tall, dark youth, "is that the light which started from Drumgrade when we were there won't reach Earth until about the year 2900."

A silence again fell upon the party while the ship went heaving gently onward and the minds of the four passengers were filled with visions of long-tailed shapes with seven-clawed hands and octopus-like sparkling tentacles. But the youth and the girl, as they went strolling apart on the dark deck, arm clasped in arm and eyes fastened upon one another, suddenly forgot that far-off world of purplish passageways, iridescent bubble palaces, and many-colored lizard lords. For them the greatest adventure still lay ahead.

www.ingramcontent.com/pod-product-compliance
Lightning Source LLC
Chambersburg PA
CBHW031256090426
42742CB00007B/485

9781434498137